MATSURI: FESTIVAL
Japanese American Celebrations and Activities

MATSURI: FESTIVAL

JAPANESE AMERICAN CELEBRATIONS AND ACTIVITIES

NANCY K. ARAKI & JANE M. HORII

HEIAN INTERNATIONAL PUBLISHING COMPANY

ISBN No. 0-89346-019-2

Third Printing, 1990
Printed in the United States of America

Heian International Inc.
P.O. Box 1013
Union city, CA 94587

Calligraphy by Reverend S. Sanada

DEDICATED TO:

LIANNE, DAVID AND KATHY

GREG AND LAUREN

CLAUDIA

JOYCE

ACKNOWLEDGEMENTS

We give our thanks and appreciation to Eiko Aoki, Lianne Araki, Craig Franklin, Ellie Fujimura Suyeda, Bertha Jenkinson, Rich Kenmotsu, Masako Moriguchi, Mak Takahashi, Marlene Tanioka and Tio Yamamoto for their support, contributions and encouragement.

We are grateful to the Reverend Koshin Ogui, former Resident Minister, San Francisco Buddhist Church, Professor Eizo Hamano, Tokyo Community College, Tokyo, Japan and Ms. Sumi Honnami, San Francisco for reviewing the various sections of the manuscript.

And special thanks to George S. Araki, for his valuable suggestions and perceptive reactions, and to each member of the Araki family for his or her unrelenting patience to see us through.

N.K.A.
J.M.H.
June 1978

CONTENTS

Page

TANGO NO SEKKU

TANABATA

OBON

PRONUNCIATION GUIDE

Japanese words are made up of syllables based on 5 fundamental vowel sounds:

a as in father
i as in ink
u as in pull
e as in bed
o as in dough

Each syllable is given equal value in pronunciation (i.e.: *MA-TSU-RI, FU-KI, SA-KU-RA*).

Long vowel sounds are written as:

ā ī ū ē ō

These should be pronounced as an elongation of the vowel. For example, *OSHŌGATSU* would be pronounced *O-SHOO-GA-TSU, KYŪSHŪ* would be pronounced *KYUU-SHUU.*

The only consonant sounds to stand alone without a vowel sound following are N and/or M (e.g.: *KOMBU, DAIKON*).

When double consonants occur, the first consonant should be pronounced as part of the first syllable and the second consonant attached to the second syllable (e.g.: *SEK/KU, TEN/NO*).

PREFACE

On March 3, 1973, Japanese Americans in San Francisco celebrated a "Community Day".* It was an unusual event where thousands of Japanese Americans milled around in good spirits to see and learn about Japanese culture as expressed through arts and crafts. A number of Japanese American groups set up booths, each with their special display and activity, and people went from one booth to another to learn to make traditional Japanese arts and craft items such as kites, fish prints, paper dolls and even the much-liked *mochi*, a confection made by agglutinizing rice.

For some people, especially older Japanese Americans, the "Community Day" activities were nostalgic, touching upon childhood memories of things they used to do and make. For others, especially younger Japanese Americans, it was foreign and yet not foreign, familiar in general, but strange in specific. And for most people, the day brought good feelings and pride in the Japanese American background.

It was on this day that we appreciated how much of the Japanese culture was being lost in America, and how much these activities had evolved through Japanese American experiences, apart from Japan.

As part of the organization we belong to, the San Francisco Center for Japanese American Studies, we had set up a booth on *Hinamatsuri* (Doll Festival). We displayed dolls made by the traditional craft of *origami* (paper folding) and taught people how to make paper dolls. We also wrote and passed out an information sheet giving a summary of the history and meaning of *Hinamatsuri*.

In writing the information sheet and in talking with people at the "Community Day" fair, we became aware that the activities were becoming less familiar with each succeeding generation of Japanese Americans. Moreover, there was no convenient source of getting such information. References were scattered, sketchy and especially remote for Japanese Americans since accounts and descriptions dealt with the celebrations as they occur in Japan. How these traditions are expressed among Japanese Americans is lacking altogether in written materials.

This book was written with the intention of providing an encapsulated history on the origin of a few Japanese traditions, especially those which have meaning for Japanese Americans. We think that in providing such information in this light, it will be more relevant to Japanese Americans as well as to general readers who are perhaps almost as much a foreigner to Japan as Japanese Americans. Working within the educational system, we also became aware of a sore need for

*In recent years "Community Day" has evolved to the *Oshōgatsu Matsuri.*

information on Asian Americans, with the emphasis on the "American" part.

We selected five Japanese cultural traditions meaningful to Japanese Americans, gathered written materials, interviewed a number of people, especially the older Japanese Americans, the *Issei* (first generation immigrants from Japan), drew upon our own personal experiences and those of Japanese American friends and from these put together this book.

We realize, too, that much of Japanese cultural activity lends itself to doing, that is making something, or dancing, or playing, or being involved in some activity. We felt that more interest and relevance could be elicited by linking together some activities to the text.

So we developed a set of activity projects to go along with each tradition, something that can be done at home or in a classroom, by young and old. These activities by themselves can provide pleasure in creating and fashioning some artistic items. They range from simple *origami* (paper folding) to learning a folk dance. Except for a few, most of the projects are new and incorporate simple, inexpensive materials available locally.

In focusing on a few Japanese traditions and how they are expressed in the United States, we hope that in some small way, we can contribute to self-understanding by Japanese Americans.

At the same time, we hope that others can come to an awareness of the Japanese American subculture. It is too easy to mistake ethnic studies as a study of a foreign culture. Such thinking reinforces the outlook that Japanese Americans are foreigners. Japanese Americans ARE Americans, ones who can contribute to cultural pluralism and to the benefit of the American society, while at the same time grow as individuals with a unique identity.

祭

MATSURI: FESTIVAL

The Japanese American community seems to have many more events or happenings throughout the year compared to other ethnic communities in our society. These events range from small group activities to larger celebrations shared with the greater community. Regardless of the magnitude of the occasion, each event can be considered part of the Japanese American legacy of MATSURI: FESTIVAL.

Matsuri is an important part of Japan and its people. The numbers and varieties of festivals attest to how deeply interwoven this expression is in the Japanese culture. Japan has been called the land of festivals; on almost any given day of the year, there is likely to be a *matsuri* at a local, regional or national level.

There are two kinds of *matsuri* in Japan. The first, solemn and worshipful, is held at various temples and shrines and at the Imperial Court. Sacred music and dance are an integral part of these ceremonial services. It is believed that *matsuri* originated in this first form when the eight myriads of gods gathered together at Ama-no-Iwato to entice the sun goddess, Amaterasu-ōmikami, out of the cave with offerings, songs and dances.

The second type of *matsuri* is in commemoration of *ujigami* (local guardian diety). The more solemn service is conducted at the shrine of the deity, followed by merrymaking by the populous. When an entire village takes part in this type of *matsuri*, it is called *furusato matsuri* (one's home village festival). *Ujigami matsuri* can be as elaborate as featuring processions in costumes with huge drawn floats paraded through the streets in a week-long celebration, to a one day neighborhood gathering with food booths, games, and vendors selling their crafts and wares. Whatever the size or style of the *matsuri*, the coming together of people, the sharing in the music, singing and dancing becomes the essential ingredient of the festivities.

The *Issei* (first generation in America; Japanese immigrant) brought with them the traditions of *matsuri*. But, by being in a different environment, the commemoration of these traditional activities became altered. To understand this transposition more clearly, let us make this analogy: perhaps one of the most traditionally accepted celebrational activities for the American Fourth of July is a picnic. This form of celebration has been passed from generation to generation. If an American were to move to Japan and continue with this picnic celebration, it would not be quite the same as in the United States because the environment would be different and the focus of the celebration by others in the new environment would be different. In the same way, the Japanese traditions of *matsuri* have been adapted to its American environment.

Matsuri exists in many forms in the Japanese American community: from *kenjin kai* (native prefecture association) events, community picnics, *mochi tsuki* (*mochi*-

making festival), temple and church bazaars and pageantries to commercial festivities like *Nisei* Week* of Los Angeles and *Aki Matsuri* (Autumn Festival) of San Francisco; community happenings like *Oshōgatsu Matsuri* (New Year's Festival), *Nihonmachi* (Japan Town) Street Fair, summer bazaars; and, *Bon Odori* (*Bon* dancing) in the various Japanese American communities.

One of the largest Japanese American festivals held each Spring is the *Sakura Matsuri* (Cherry Blossom Festival). The San Francisco Bay Area community joins in this colorful two week celebration that brings people together to commemorate the coming of Spring symbolized by the cherry blossoms, and to enjoy the traditions of Japanese performing and martial arts. Special cultural demonstrations and exhibits such as *ikebana* (flower arrangement), *bonsai* (miniature trees), *origami* (paper folding), *cha no yu* (tea ceremony) and *shodō* (calligraphy) are also offered. The *matsuri* ends with a Grand Parade of dancers, musicians, marchers, floats and features a *taru mikoshi* (barrel of *sake* on a carrying platform), which is so huge it takes several dozens of young people to carry it on their shoulders. The huge barrel is hoisted up and down as they parade along the streets to the cries of *washoi*!** Whether one is an active participant or on-looker, the Japanese tradition of *matsuri* continues with good feelings of camaraderie among Japanese Americans and members of the larger community in sharing this legacy.

There are five *matsuri* which are probably familiar to most Japanese Americans: *Oshōgatsu* (New Year's), *Hinamatsuri* (Girls' Day), *Tango No Sekku* (Boys' Day), *Tanabata* (Star Festival), *Bon Odori* (Bon dance). We explore these festivals in the following pages from their historical Japanese roots to the adapted Japanese American expressions.

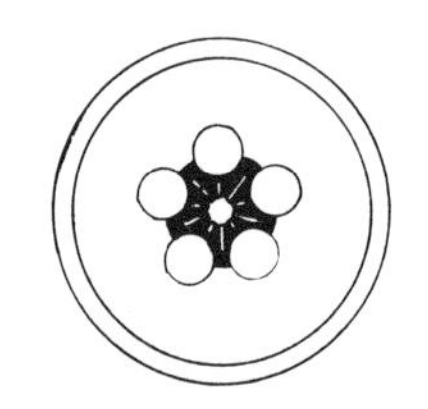

*Second generation Japanese American.

**As in "Heave Ho!"

正月

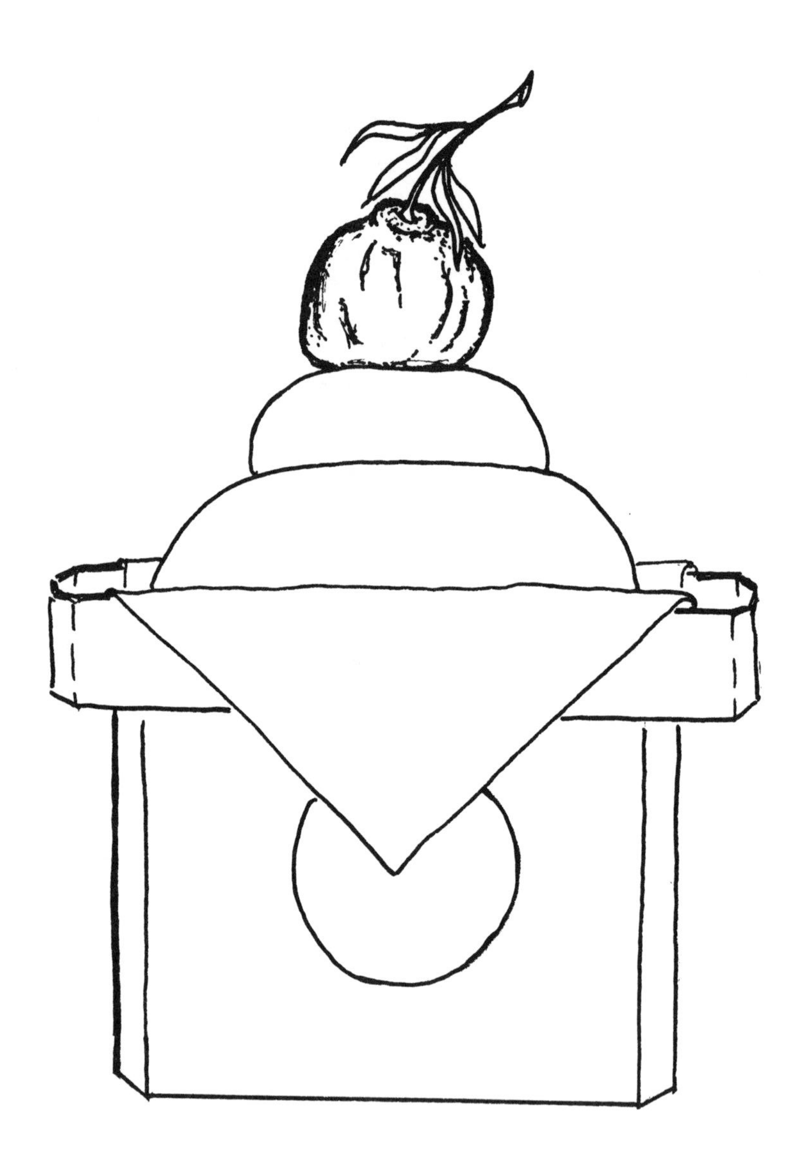

OSHŌGATSU

Shinnen akemashite omedetō gozaimasu.
(New Year has opened, it is to be congratulated!)

Shinnen omedetō gozaimasu.
(Happy New Year!)

For Japanese, *Oshōgatsu* (New Year; literally, new month) is the most important celebration of the year, a festive occasion with good feelings and nostalgia. Many Japanese Americans, in the same way, honor the New Year, but as it is for most Americans, Christmas is also very much celebrated.

For one reason or another, *Issei* readily adopted the Christmas celebration even though most of them lacked the religious background for it. In the holiday spirit, greeting cards are sent, presents exchanged and trees decorated by most Japanese Americans. Why did adoption of a Christian and foreign practice so readily happen among early *Issei*? Several reasons might be offered.

First, the Japanese characteristic of adaptability is well known. Second, the pressure and the desire to adapt to the greater American society were great. Third, and perhaps most important, some Christmas activities resemble some of the *Issei*'s own traditions which they had carried with them from Japan. For example, *oseibo* is a custom in which gifts are given at the end of the year in gratitude for past kindness and favors; *otoshidama* are envelopes containing money given to children at New Year's; exchanging of *nenga* or *nenshi* (New Year's cards) was a popular custom in the early Meiji Era (1868-1912); and, *kadomatsu* is a decoration made of pine branches and bamboo to adorn the entrances of Japanese homes during the New Year's season. With these and other customs highlighting the New Year's period, incorporating Christmas customs was very easily accomplished.

So for Japanese Americans, the holiday season is only half over with Christmas, since New Year's is next. The house must be cleaned of the clutter and dust of the past year to start the New Year afresh. Preparation of food for New Year's also occupies much time. Groceries must be bought and the cooking requires several days. Some families and groups gather together to make *mochi* in a traditional *mochi tsuki* (*mochi* making event). On New Year's Eve, many go to parties and revel in the American style. Chances are that the older folks who stay at home might watch the television broadcast of New Year's Eve in Times Square before turning out the old year. *Toshikoshi soba* (end of year buckwheat noodles) is eaten by some Japanese Americans. But, it is New Year's day that is the important occasion. It may begin with the family gathering to toast the New Year with *sake*, with children taking a token sip of the rice wine, and eating the traditional bowl of *ozōni* (a soup with *mochi* in it). After partaking of soup and other foods specifically prepared for the day, the family may go visiting relatives and friends to wish them a good year, or get ready to receive guests who will come throughout the day. At each home visited, New Year's greetings are exchanged and guests are offered quantities of food and drink. There might be watching football on television, playing cards, or other games, but food is central.

It is no wonder that Japanese Americans associate *Oshōgatsu* with food. And the food is special, such as *osechi ryōri** (boiled vegetable dish), a must for New Year's. In Japan, *osechi ryōri* is served only for New Year's, but here in the United States, Japanese Americans may serve it at any festive gathering such as parties, family picnics and other holidays.

Along with the *osechi ryōri* and other traditional New Year's foods, the Japanese Americans prepare an array of Japanese foods, such as *tempura* (deep fried prawns and vegetables), *sushi* (sweet vinegared rice in various forms), and *teriyaki* (meats marinated and broiled in soy sauce and sugar). And a twist unheard of in Japan is serving "typical" American foods such as turkey, ham, jello mold, and even dishes from other Asian countries such as Chinese chicken salad and *char siu* (barbecued sweet pork).

The Japanese American style of the New Year's celebration, the cleaning, cooking and the socializing, have their roots in Japan, of course, but it differs from the Japanese style. The Japanese American New Year is a mixture of Japanese traditions and casual American pastimes.

In Japan, the New Year's season is much more involved and extends for several days. In earlier times, the celebration lasted the entire first month. The Japanese New Year's celebration evolved out of rituals associated with the changes of season, which is of utmost importance in Japanese farming.

In olden times, Japanese New Year was held in conjunction with the passing of *daikan* (the Great Cold) and the coming of Spring. According to modern calendar, this period falls between January 6-21. But in olden days, another calendar was used. The *kyūreki* (old or lunar calendar) was based on movements of the sun and moon and corresponded so well to the seasonal changes in Japan, that even today, farmers use the old calendar. The *shinreki* or *seireki* (new or Western calendar) was adopted in the Meiji Era (1873), so that now the New Year is celebrated at the same time as in the Western world.

Special housecleaning may have come during the Tokugawa Period (1603-1868),

**Osechi ryōri*: *Takenoko* (bamboo shoots), *shiitake* (dried mushrooms), *gobō* (burdock root), *renkon* (lotus root), *sato-imo* (taro), *daikon* (long white radish), *fuki* (coltsfoot), string beans, carrots—cooked in broth, seasoned with soy sauce and sugar.

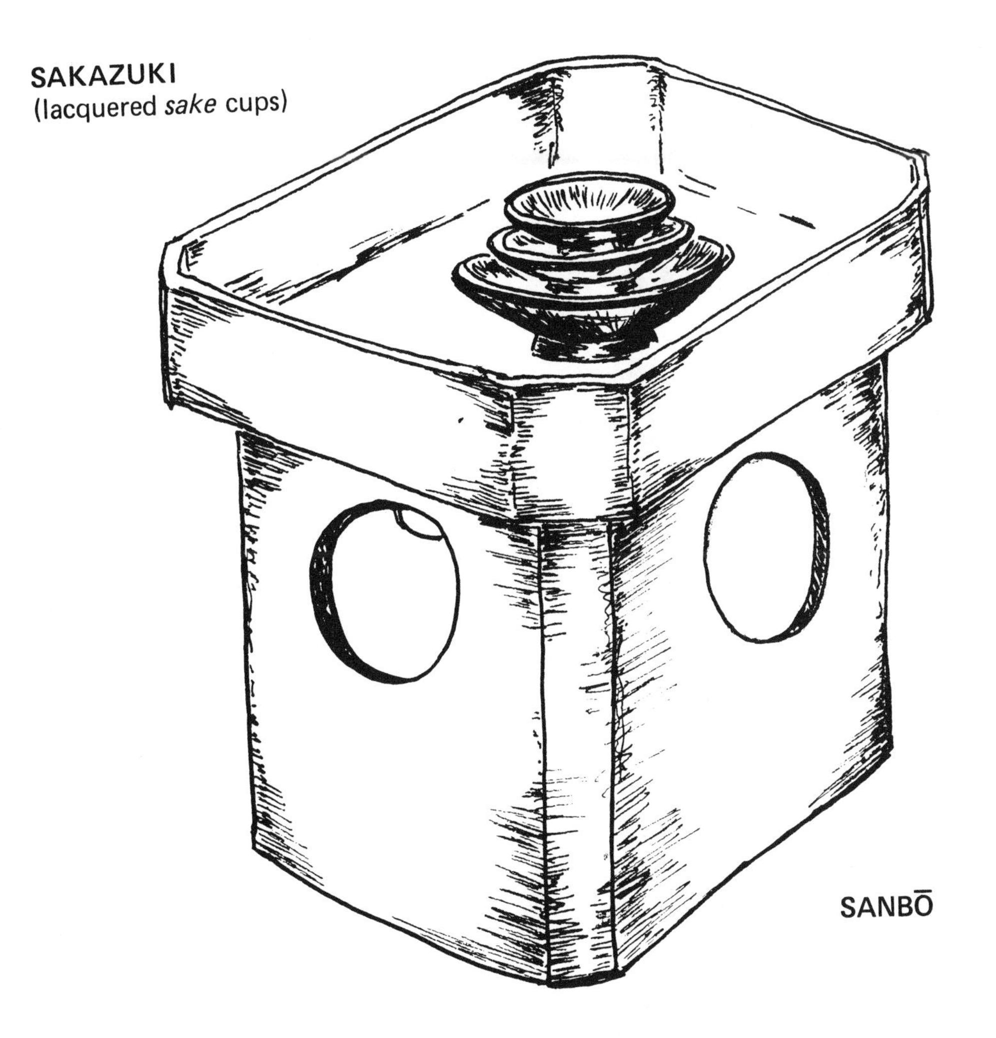
SAKAZUKI
(lacquered *sake* cups)
SANBŌ

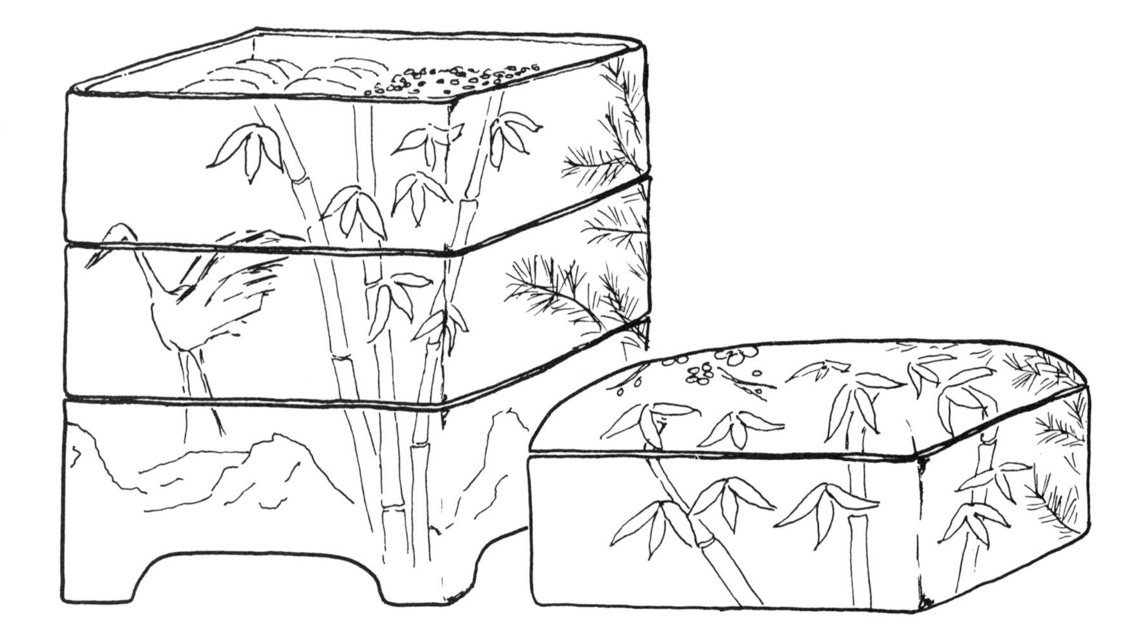

JŪBAKO

when an official cleaning period called *susu-barai* (soot sweeping) was set aside, beginning on the 13th day of the last month of the year. This type of housecleaning, with special attention paid to the kitchen, is found in other cultures (e.g., the homage paid to the kitchen god in the Chinese culture).

Today, New Year housecleaning is done up to the last minute. Cooking, as well as housecleaning, was forbidden during the first few days of the New Year with the thought that good spirits should not be disturbed or swept out. Food which can keep for several days, such as *osechi ryōri* (New Year's food; boiled vegetables), are prepared. In the larger cities and communities, delicatessan stores make and sell *osechi ryōri. Osechi* is a surprisingly plain food, not elaborate as might be expected for the most important Japanese festival. Like most foods, *osechi* varies from region to region and family to family. Along with the *osechi ryōri, kuchitori* (side dishes), *sunomono* (vinegared, salad-type dishes), and boiled or roasted fish are prepared. These dishes are placed in a *jūbako* (square container made of porcelain or lacquerware, three to four stacks high, with cover on top); these dishes are collectively called *jūzume ryōri* (stacked, cold dishes).

To start the New Year with a clean slate, all debts are paid and disputes and differences are settled. *Bōnen kai* (year-end parties) are held by businesses, clubs and friends to promote goodwill and to patch up past misunderstandings. The idea of starting afresh is the dominant theme. Symbols of the reawakening of nature are also prominent in the celebration of the New Year: plants, fruits, flowers, all emphasizing rebirth, newness and fertility.

With the house and soul in order, *toshi-koshi soba* (end of year buckwheat noodles) is eaten, and as it nears midnight, the *joya no kane* (end of the year bell) toll 108 times from nearby Buddhist temples. The tolls represent the leaving behind of 108 worldly concerns of the old year. The last boom of the *joya no kane* is struck at midnight, and a new beginning has dawned.

The New Year starts fresh with people giving thanks for the past and expressing hope for a greater, happier new year. It is felt that the very first day sets the pace for the rest of the year and should be filled with much gaity and joy to get the right start. Wearing new clothing, *kimono* and *obi*, family members join in a toast for good fortune with *otoso* (sweet *sake* brewed with cinnamon and other spices), which is believed to prevent sickness in general. *Sake* (rice wine) is also served. Three *sakazuki* (lacquered *sake* cups, graded in size) are stacked and placed on a *sanbō* (tray stand). These cups represent Heaven, Earth and Human being, and every member of the family takes three sips from each cup.

Ozōni (soup with *mochi*), another traditional food of the day, originated during the Muromachi Era (1392-1490) as part of the New Year's fare. The taste and types of *ozōni* vary from region to region. *Ozōni* is also eaten on happy occasions such as weddings.

Games are very much a part of New Year's day. Card games like *hanafuda* (flower-card game) and *karutatori* (100 poem matching game) are played by the whole family. Girls like to play *hanetsuki*, a Japanese badminton game played with a *hagoita* (battledore) and *hane* (shuttlecock), and a game called *temari*, bouncing balls to rhyming verses, while boys enjoy flying *tako* (kites) and spinning *koma* (tops).

During the first 3 to 4 days of the New Year, the Japanese visit relatives and friends and go to temples and shrines. To accommodate the numerous temple and shrine-goers, metropolitan trains run all night on New Year's Eve. During this time, many people wear the traditional *kimono* clothing and Japan takes on the appearance of what the foreigner expects of Japan.

Many symbols appear at New Year's: *kadomatsu* (corner pine; an arrangement of pine and bamboo) is put up at the start of the New Year season to ward off evil dominance, invoke fertility and growth, and to bring worldly blessings to the house. The *matsu* (pine) symbolizes constancy, morality, and the power to resist adversity and old age. The pine needles are excellent for exorcism since it is believed that ghosts and evil spirits dislike sharp points. Another feature of the pine needles is that they occur in pairs, joined at the ends, to symbolize wedded love and unity. The *take* (bamboo) symbolizes great strength and its green color denotes vitality. *Shida* (fern) is sometimes used in the arrangement to symbolize vigor and progeny.

KADOMATSU

Shimenawa (sacred rope) has its origin with the sun-goddess, Amaterasu-ōmikami, who withdrew into a rocky cave and refused to come out to shine on the Plain of High Heaven and on the eight myriads of gods. After using much magic and strategy, the gods managed to get the goddess out of the cave, and they stretched a *shimenawa* across the cave entrance so that she would not be able to reenter. Although the *shimenawa* was originally meant to keep a benevolent goddess from going away, it has become interpreted over the years to keeping out the evil spirits of illness and impurity. It is believed that no evil can pass beyond the line of the *shimenawa* and consequently, when used, it sanctifies the place or thing around which it is placed.

Wànawa (circle rope; sacred rope of New Year) is a modern version of the *shimenawa*. During the New Year season, the rope is placed on the *tokonoma* (alcove) or a sacred place in the Japanese home, as well as at the front entrance of the house.

Mochi (pounded rice cake) is one food item which is always part of the Japanese New Year. *Mochi* is a special kind of steamed rice which has been pounded into a sticky, pasty state. It is then shaped into small, round buns. *Mochi* was originally made as offerings to *kami* (gods) at shrines. This offering was then cut into small pieces and given to people for good health and fortune. Later, the *mochi* came to be eaten on various festive occasions and during the Heian Era (794-1192), it became an integral part of the New Year feast.

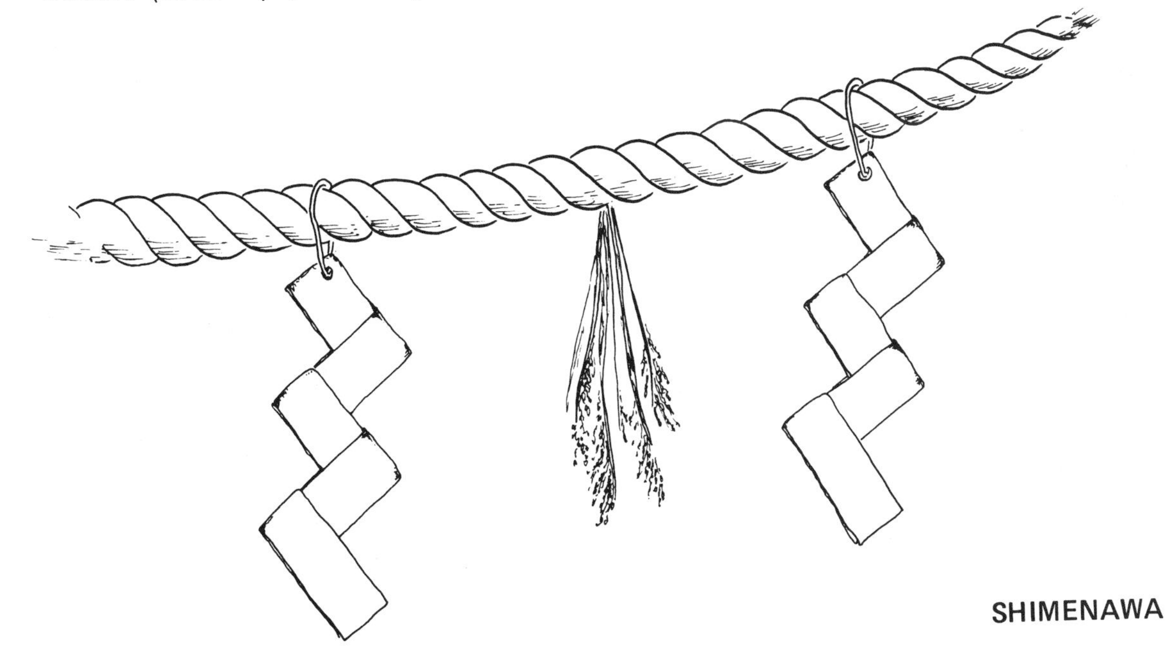

SHIMENAWA

Mochi offered to the gods is called *kagami mochi*, or mirrored *mochi*. It is composed of a large, round, white, bun-shaped *mochi* with a smaller one stacked on top. *Kagami mochi* is placed on a white paper in the center of a tray stand, the *sanbō*. The origin of this offering is based on Amaterasu-ōmikami's (sun-goddess) hiding in the cave of Ama-no-Iwato. With the sun-goddess in hiding, the world became dark and prayers for her reappearance were made to a mirror, which symbolized the goddess. The *kagami mochi* represents the mirror and is a symbol of hope for a brighter and happier New Year.

The *kagami mochi* is sometimes embellished with other New Year's symbols: *shida* (fern) for progeny; *kobu* or *konbu* (kelp), symbol of joy because the word is found in *yorokobu* (to be glad); *dai-dai* (bigarde, type of orange, although the *mikan*, mandarin orange, is presently used) meaning generation to generation; *umizarigani* (lobster) or *ise ebi* (spiny or spring lobster), symbolizing longevity ("may you live so long as to have your back bend as the lobster's") and a wish for a more prosperous future symbolized by the red color of the cooked shellfish; and, *kaki* (persimmon) or *hoshigaki* (dried persimmon) which stands for fecundity and happy family. The words *kakikomu* or *kakiatsumeru* mean to rake in, to accumulate, to become prosperous.

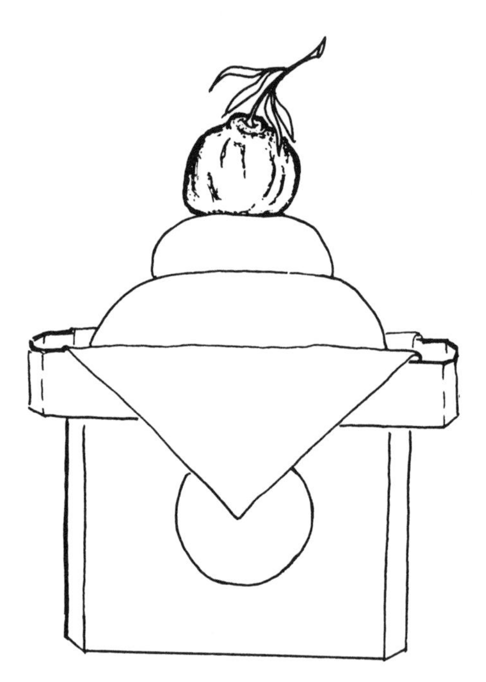

KAGAMI MOCHI

Shōchikubai, an arrangement combining *matsu* (pine), *ume* (plum blossom) and *take* (bamboo) stands for the New Year and one's wish for happiness. This motif is used to decorate many artistic and utilitarian objects during *Oshōgatsu*. The *ume* represents the feminine and *matsu*, the masculine, while the bamboo indicates strength. The plum blossoms also connote bravery for blooming while the snow still covers the ground.

The *tsuru* (crane) and *kame* (tortoise) are other symbols of longevity. According to legends, the *tsuru* lives for a thousand years, while the *kame* lives for ten thousand years.

Although paper cranes are folded year round, they are hung in homes at *Oshōgatsu* as symbols of good fortune and long life. *Tsuru*-inspired designs on dishes, containers and trays, as well as other articles, are used during this festival.

Foods also take on special meaning. The *tai* (sea bream) is roasted whole, with its body arched to form a circle, and is considered good luck because its name is contained in the word *omedetai* (congratulatory). *Mame* (beans) symbolizes good health, and *kazunoko* (herring roe) means "numerous children" or many progeny.

SHŌCHIKUBAI

MATSU (pine)

TAKE (bamboo)

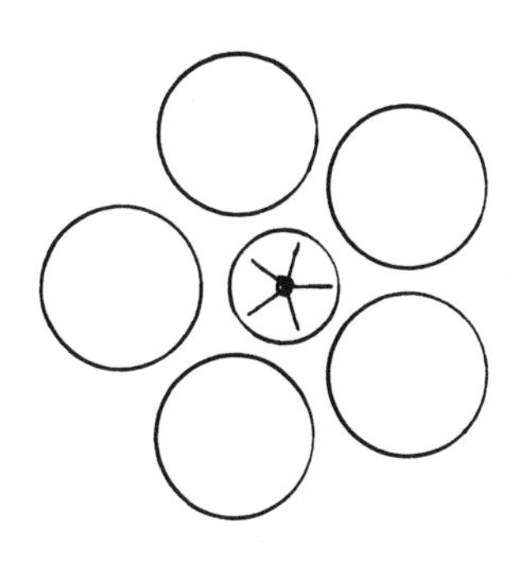

UME (plum blossom)

MOCHI TSUKI

MOCHI TSUKI

In earlier times, *mochi tsuki* (*mochi*-making event) was an important part of the New Year's celebration. In the rural areas, family and relatives gathered to pound *mochi* together, while in the cities, traveling *mochi tsuki* men would come with all their equipment to pound *mochi* for the households. Today, *mochi tsuki* is done by some shrines and rural families. Most everywhere else, mechanized pounding machines have taken the place of human power and people simply order *mochi* from confectionery stores.

Similarly, in the United States, *mochi* is made by the various Japanese American confectionery stores, and only a few families and groups gather together for a *mochi tsuki*. Recently, there has been a growing interest in making *mochi* the "old-fashioned" way, like the *Issei* used to do several decades ago.

The paraphernalia for *mochi tsuki* consists of *usu* (mortars made of wood stumps, stone or concrete forms), *kine* (pestles or wooden mallets), and *seiro* (rice steaming frames). The *mochigome* (sweet glutinous rice) is washed the night before and left to soak in water in large kettles or tubs. The water is drained off and the *mochigome* is placed into a *seiro*, which consists of a wooden frame holding a bamboo mat. Three or four *seiro* are stacked on top of each other and placed on top of a boiling kettle. In time, the *seiro* nearest the kettle is removed and the steam-cooked rice is dumped into a warmed *usu*. A fresh *seiro* with *mochigome* is placed on top of the stack.

Using the wooden mallets, two persons push down on the rice in the *usu* for a short time until the rice forms a single mass. Then the pounding begins. One person, sometimes two in turns, swings a wooden mallet in great arcs and pounds the rice with even force and enthusiasm. Another person quickly darts his or her hand into the *usu* and moves the rice into position for the next rhythmic pound. The pounding continues for several minutes until the mass is smooth and shiny, and individual grains of rice are no longer discernible. It is now a large mass of *mochi*.

The *mochi* is lifted out (still very hot) onto a cloth or paper-covered table on which a thin layer of *mochiko* (sweet rice flour), has been spread. *Mochiko* is spread on the surface of the sticky *mochi* in order to make it easier to handle. One person pinches off small portions about the size of golf balls, and passes them to others who form them into the flattened-round bun shapes with their hands. Finished *mochi* are set aside for drying.

Freshly pounded *mochi*, without the *mochiko*, is quite tasty when eaten with a garnish made of *daikon oroshi* (long, white radish, grated fine) mixed with *goma* (sesame seeds) and *shōyu* (soy sauce). It can also be eaten with a sauce of *shōyu* and *nori* (seaweed) or a mixture of sugar, salt and *kinako* (soybean flour).

Mochi is frequently roasted so that it puffs up and becomes crisp on the outside, while the inside is soft and sticky. It is also boiled in water to soften, then eaten with the various sauces. *Mochi* is also put into soups, as in the traditional *ozōni* and *zenzai* (sweet, red *azuki* bean soup with hull) or *shiruko* (smooth, sweet red *azuki* bean soup).

Mochi, which is not eaten in a few days, may be stored in the freezer and, if packaged properly, will last for months. Fresh *mochi* can also be sliced very thin, dried and stored in airtight containers. These strips of hard dried *mochi* are deep-fried to make *kakimochi* (puffy rice cracker) which is seasoned with salt, sugar or rolled in *satōjōyu* (sugar and soy sauce, boiled to a syrup).

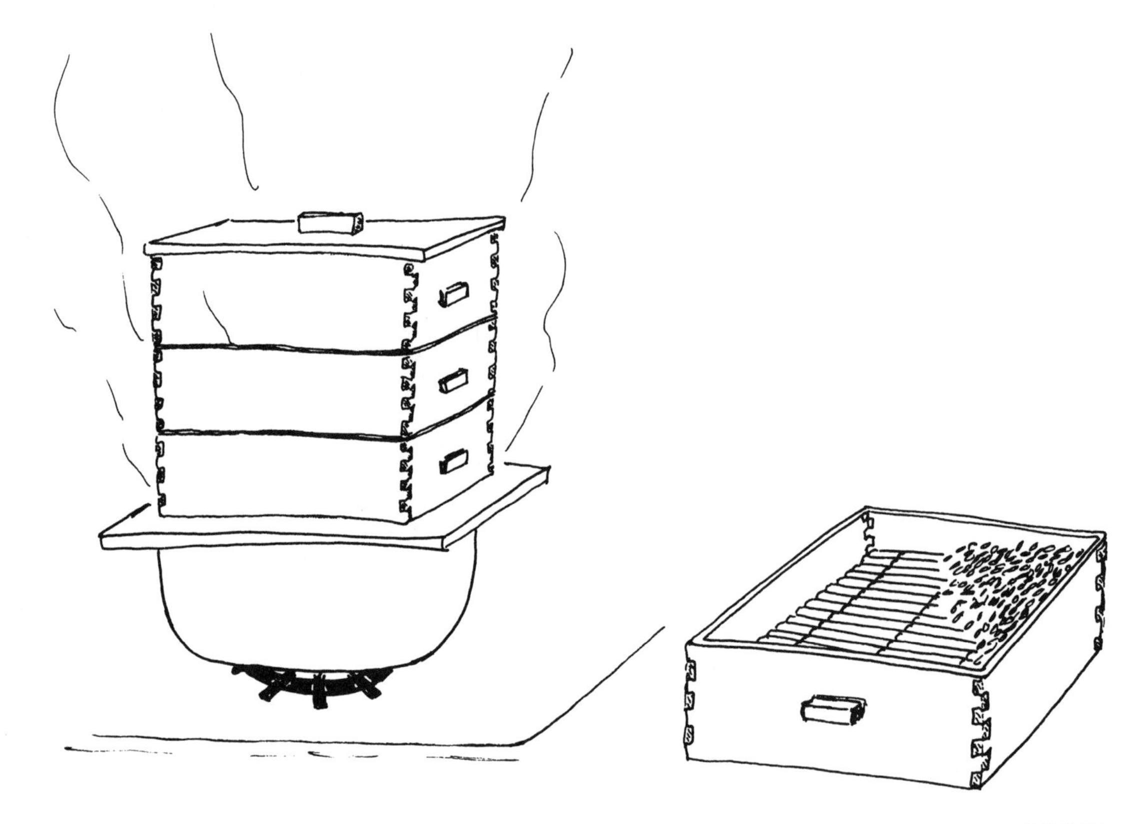

SEIRO

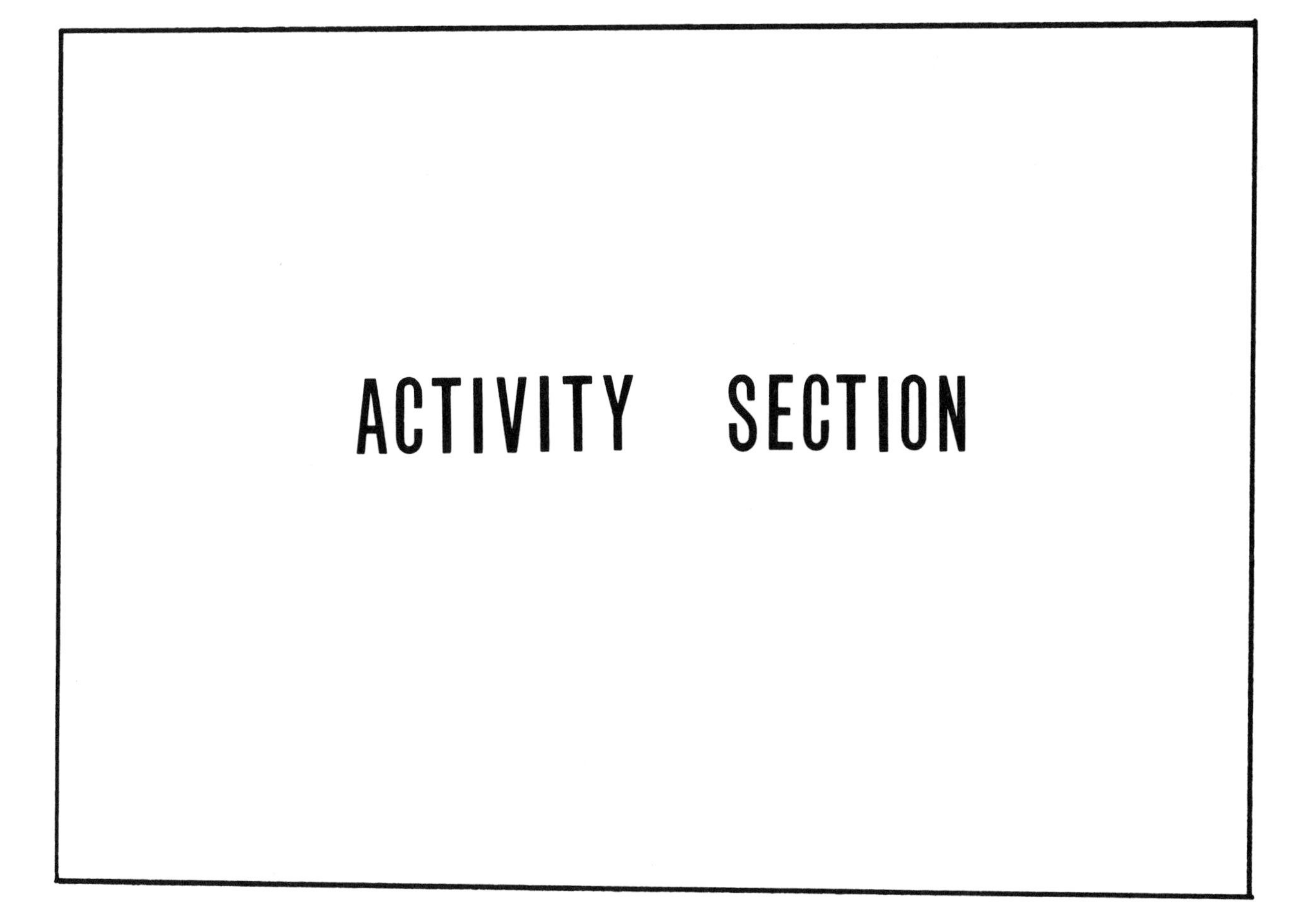
ACTIVITY SECTION

OSHŌGATSU

Instructions are given for making three popular symbols of *Oshōgatsu*: *tsuru* (crane), *umizarigani* (lobster), and *daruma* (self-uprighting doll). Also, since food is important to the Japanese American celebration, recipes are given for a few simple dishes typically prepared for *Oshōgatsu*. The ingredients can be obtained at local Japanese American or Asian American food stores.

The crane and lobster are made by *origami* (paper folding). Materials needed are:

- *Origami* paper, or any paper cut into squares (fadeless colored paper, gift wrapping paper). Avoid thick or very thin paper because it will be difficult to make folds.
- Scissors and colored felt tip pens or colored pencils (for lobster only).

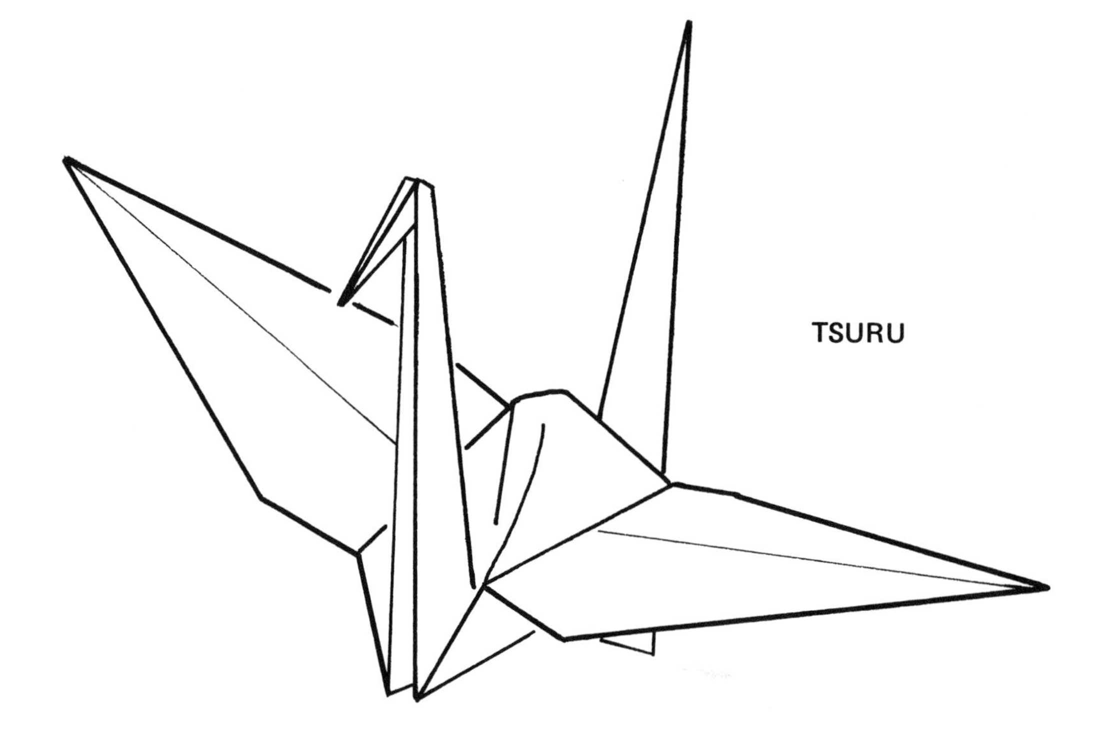

TSURU

TSURU (crane)

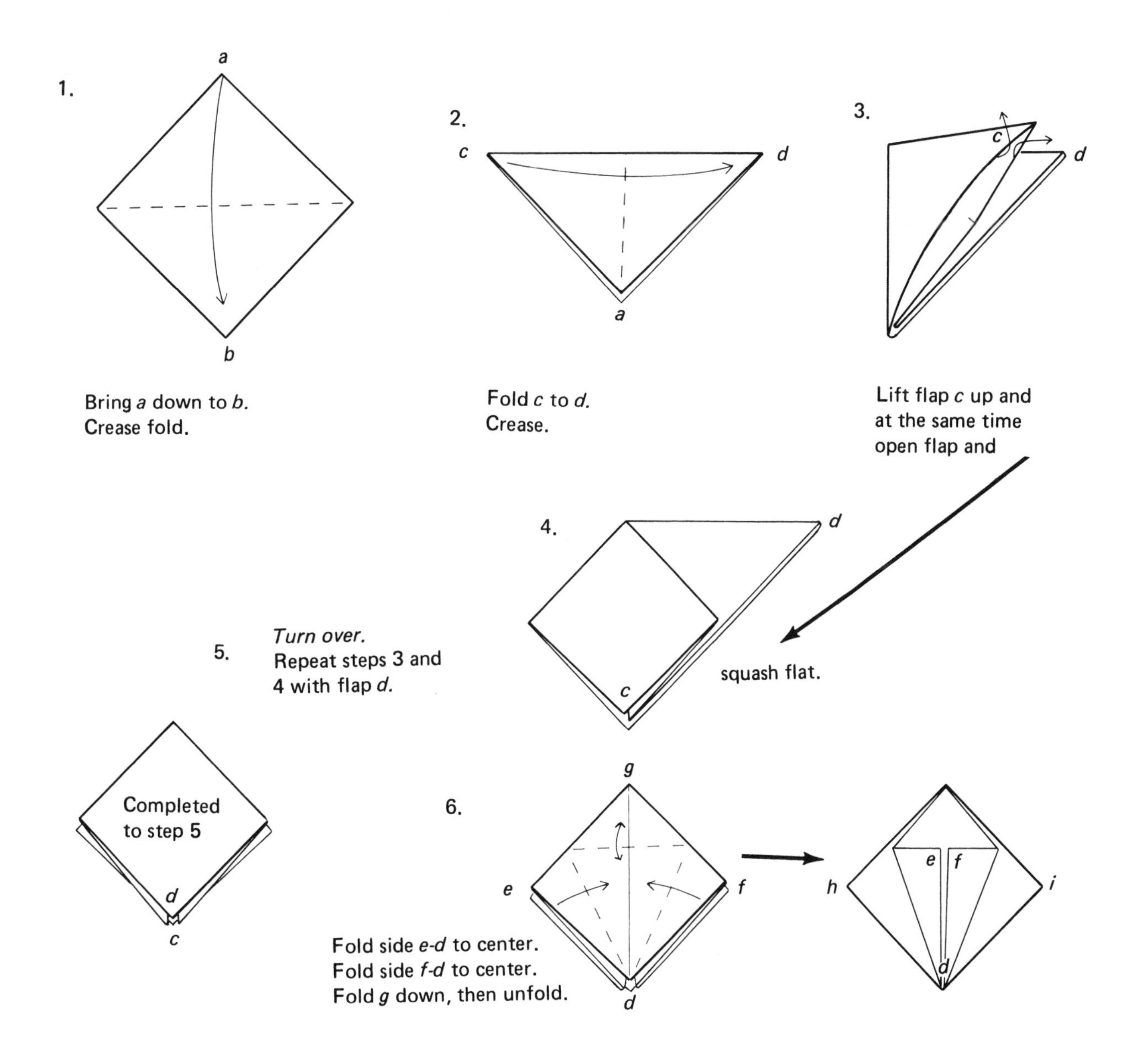
1.
a
b
Bring *a* down to *b*.
Crease fold.
2.
c
d
a
Fold *c* to *d*.
Crease.
3.
c
d
Lift flap *c* up and
at the same time
open flap and
squash flat.
4.
d
c
5.
Turn over.
Repeat steps 3 and
4 with flap *d*.
Completed
to step 5
d
c
6.
g
e
f
d
Fold side *e-d* to center.
Fold side *f-d* to center.
Fold *g* down, then unfold.
h
e
f
i
d

7.

Turn over.
Repeat step 6
with sides *h* and *i.*

8.

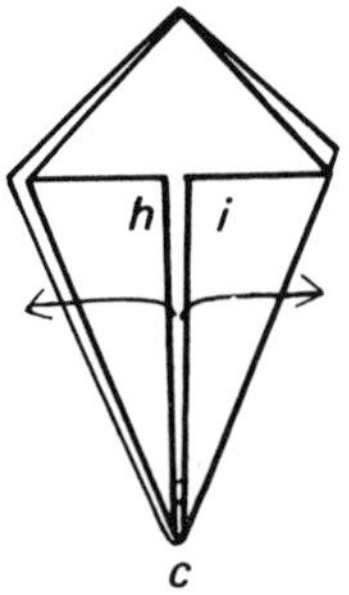

Open flaps *h* and *i*
outward.

9.

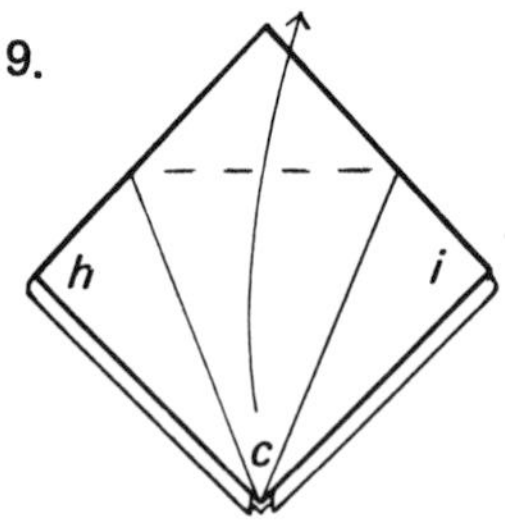

Lift *c* upward and
at the same time

10.

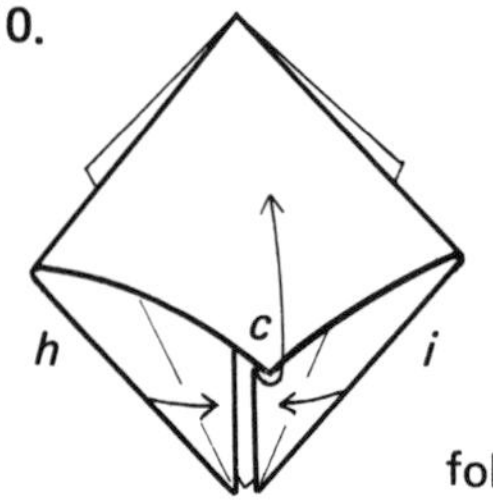

fold *h* and *i* inward.

11.

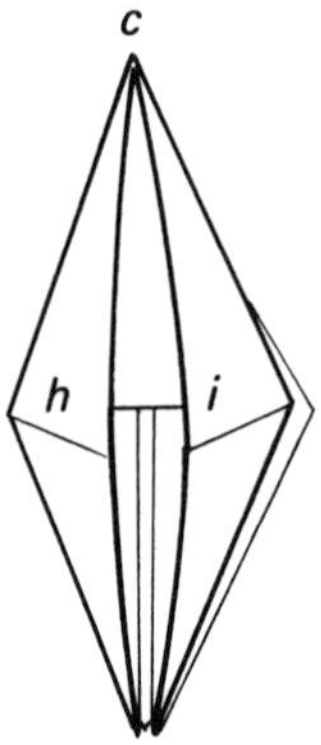

Press flat.

12.

Turn over.
Repeat steps 8-11
with flap *d.*

13.

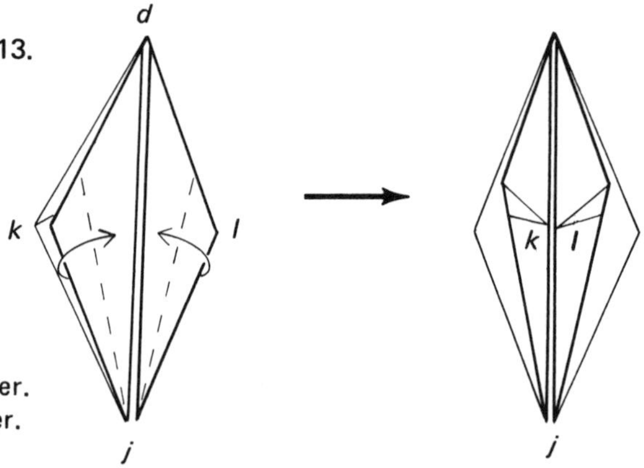

Fold side *k-j* to center.
Fold side *l-j* to center.

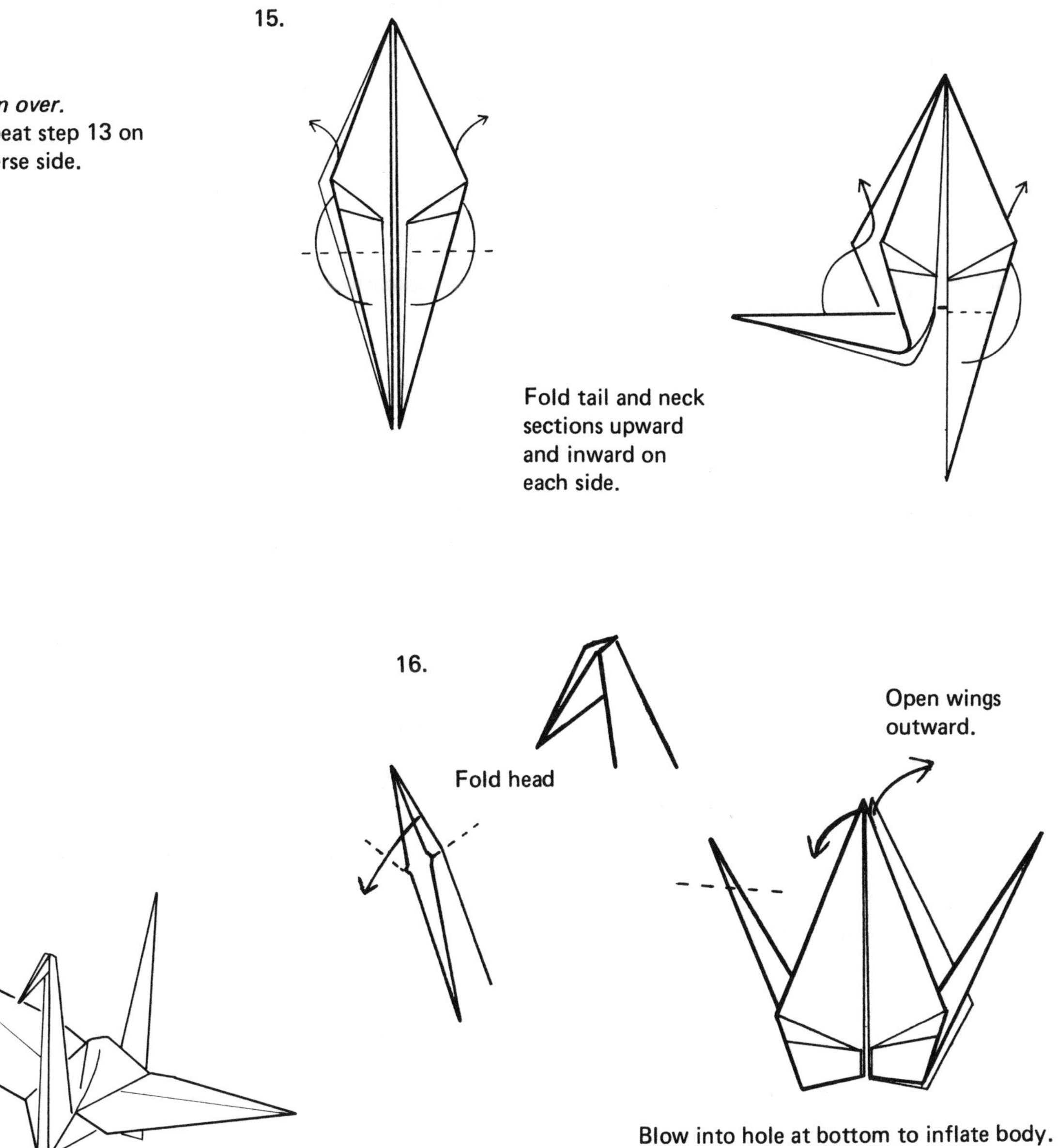
14.
Turn over.
Repeat step 13 on
reverse side.
15.
Fold tail and neck
sections upward
and inward on
each side.
16.
Fold head
Open wings
outward.
Blow into hole at bottom to inflate body.

UMIZARIGANI (lobster)

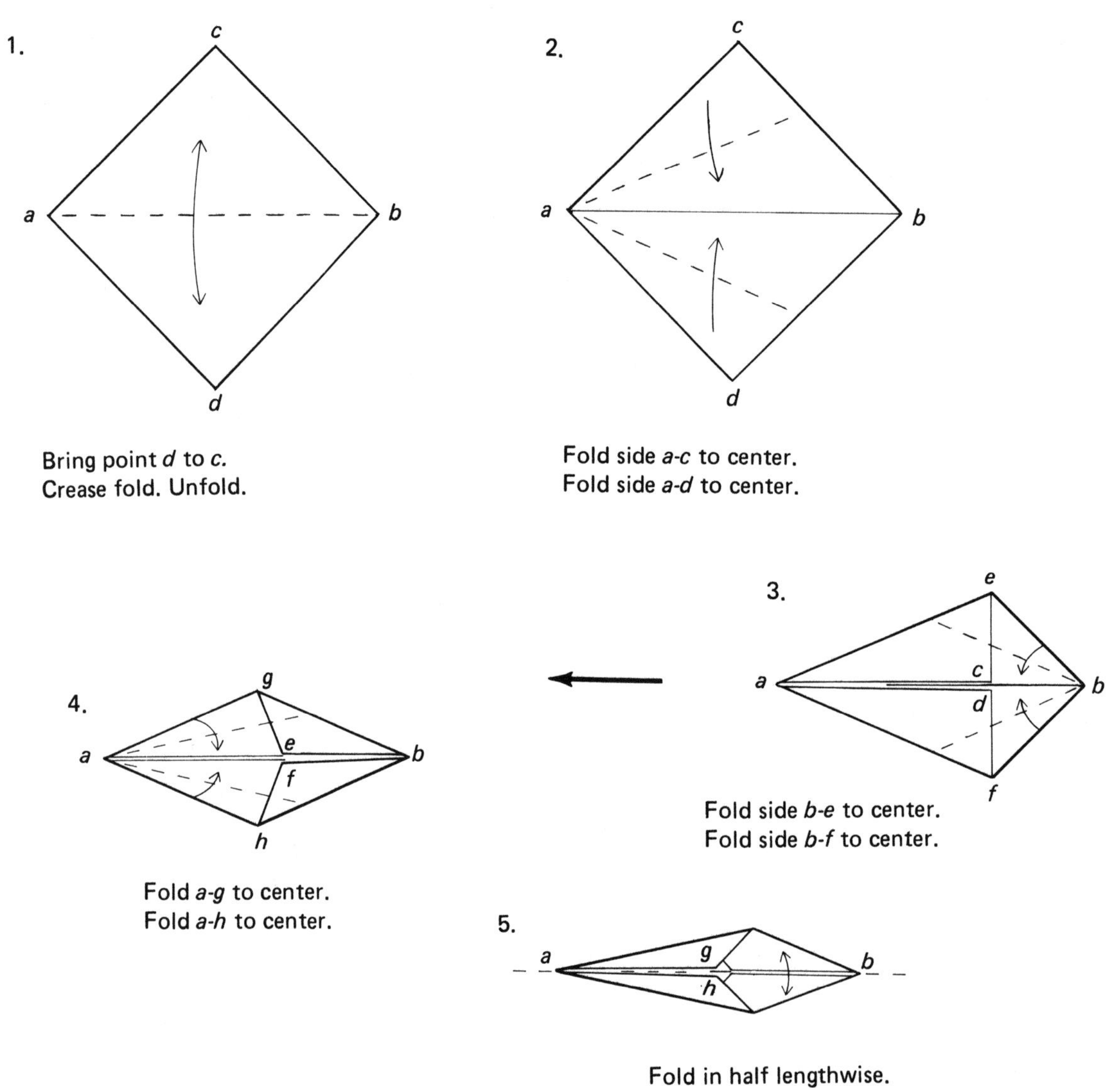

1. Bring point *d* to *c*.
Crease fold. Unfold.

2. Fold side *a-c* to center.
Fold side *a-d* to center.

3. Fold side *b-e* to center.
Fold side *b-f* to center.

4. Fold *a-g* to center.
Fold *a-h* to center.

5. Fold in half lengthwise.
Unfold.

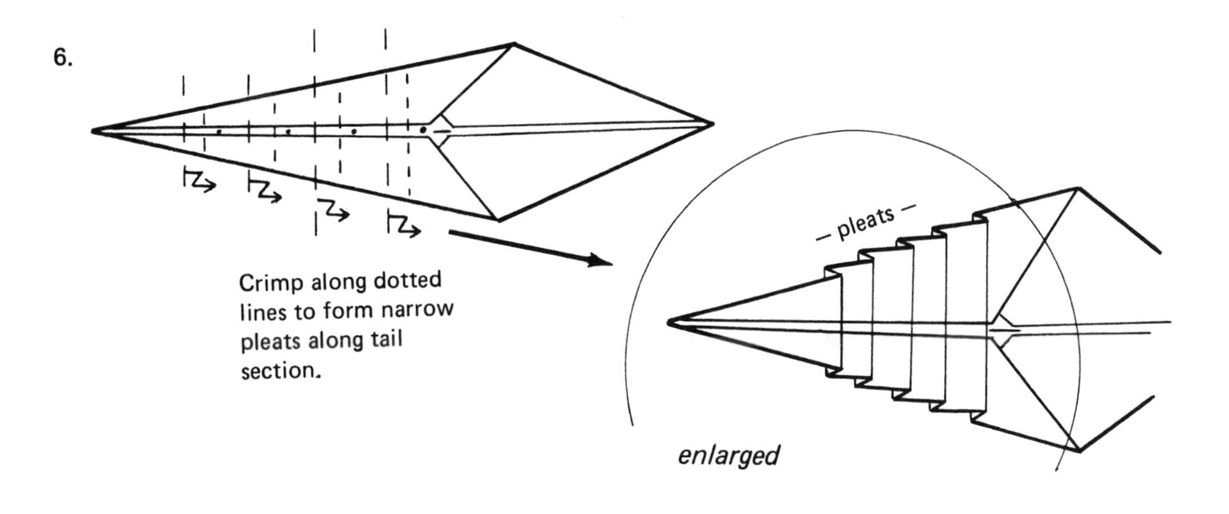
6.
Crimp along dotted lines to form narrow pleats along tail section.
– pleats –
enlarged

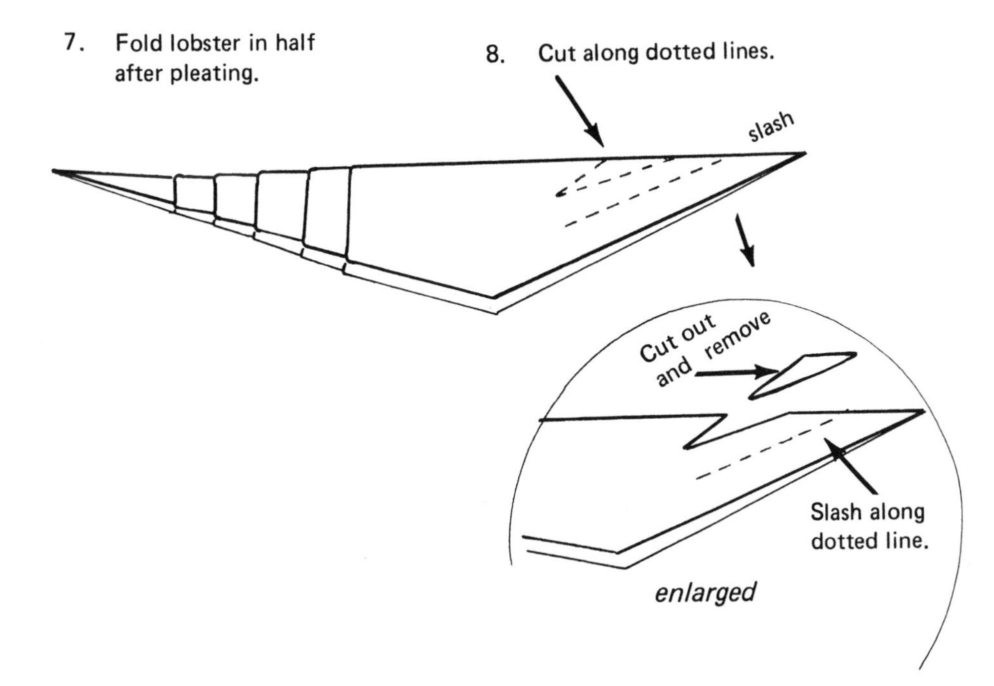
7. Fold lobster in half after pleating.
8. Cut along dotted lines.
slash
Cut out and remove
Slash along dotted line.
enlarged

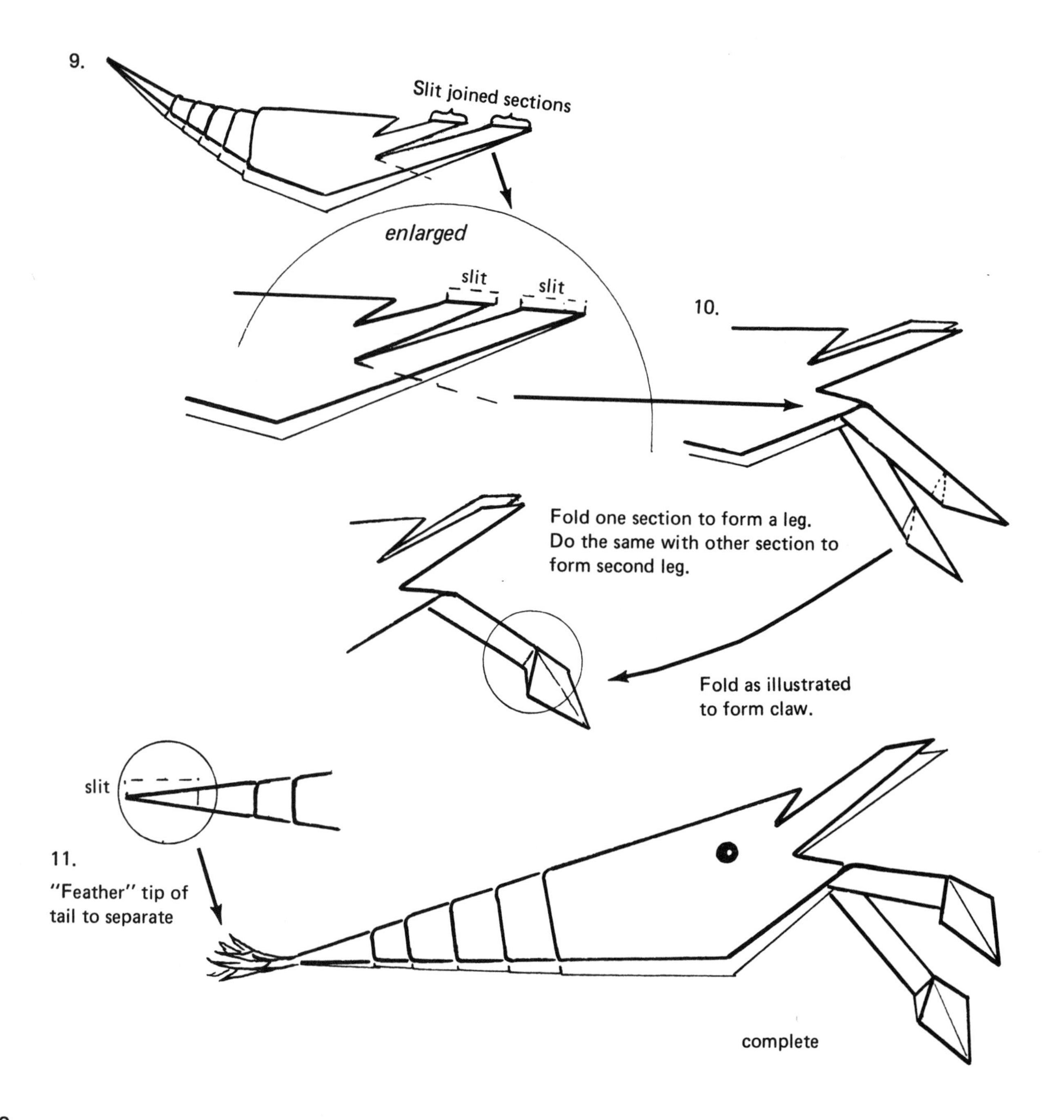
9.
Slit joined sections
enlarged
slit
slit
10.
Fold one section to form a leg.
Do the same with other section to
form second leg.
Fold as illustrated
to form claw.
slit
11.
"Feather" tip of
tail to separate
complete

DARUMA

DARUMA

The *daruma* is a good luck charm which many people in Japan purchase during the beginning of the New Year with hopes that it will bring good fortune.

This popular doll comes in many sizes and is created from a variety of materials, including wood, clay, rocks, and *papier-mâché.* The most popular and commonly seen *daruma* is made of *papier-mâché* and has a weighted, rounded bottom so that it will return to an upright position no matter how often it is knocked down. This persistence to return upright is considered an admirable trait.

The facial characteristics of the *daruma* differs from region to region. Most commonly, the *daruma* is painted red all over, with the exception of the face, and has two prominent eyes. Some *daruma* dolls have blank eyes without the iris, showing only the whites.

This type is used for making a wish. One iris is painted on with the wish,

and when the wish comes true, the other iris is painted in.

The *daruma* gets its name from the Indian Buddhist priest, named Bodhidharma. The story goes that Bodhidharma sat facing a cliff in silent meditation for nine years. The lack of movement caused him to lose the use of his arms and legs, but in spite of this disability, he went throughout China with his teachings. This particular source of inner strength and determination is represented by the *daruma* doll.

PAPIER-MÂCHÉ DARUMA
(Self-righting type)

Overview for making DARUMA: (approximately the size of a large grapefruit)

	Step I	Step II	Step III	Step IV
	Making basic form ↓	Applying weighted base ↓	Framing facial features ↓	Finishing ↓
Media:	papier-mâché ↓	plaster of Paris ↓	paper construction and papier-mâché ↓	painting ↓
Materials:	plastic sandwich bag Scotch tape wheat paste water bowl newspaper (including comic section, or any section with a different color)	125 grams (¼ lb.) dry plaster of Paris 120ml (½ C.) water container (anything which can be discarded) plastic knife (smooth edged) or spoon	newspaper Scotch tape wheat paste bowl lightweight cardboard, index card or tagboard	poster paint, red and flesh colors lacquer or shellac

PAPIER-MÂCHÉ DARUMA

Step I: Making the Basic Form

Form:

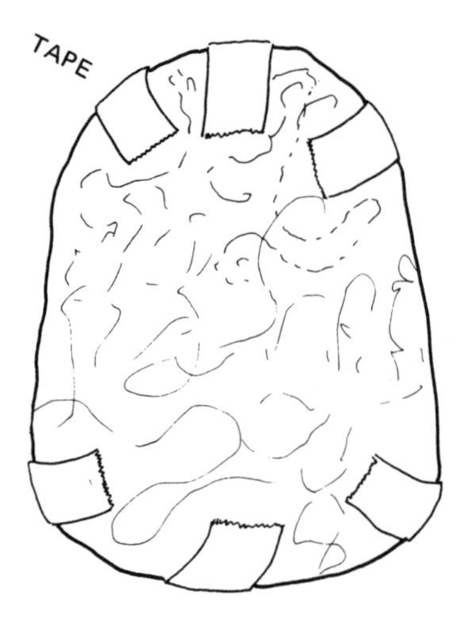

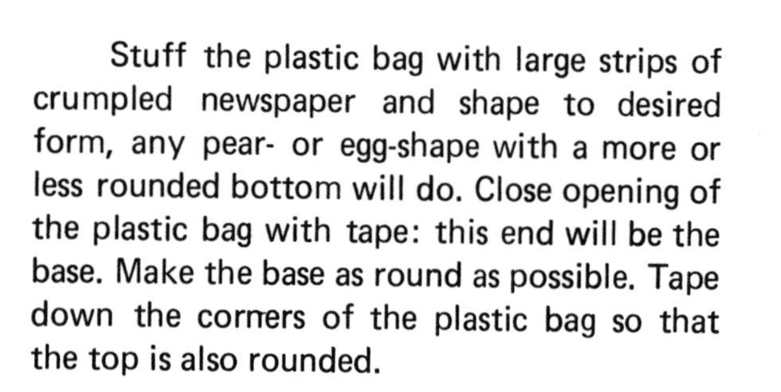

Stuff the plastic bag with large strips of crumpled newspaper and shape to desired form, any pear- or egg-shape with a more or less rounded bottom will do. Close opening of the plastic bag with tape: this end will be the base. Make the base as round as possible. Tape down the corners of the plastic bag so that the top is also rounded.

Papier Mâché:

1) Mix the wheat paste with water, making a watery paste.

2) Tear the newspaper into strips, about 4cm (1-1/2 inches) wide and 20cm (8 inches) long. Dip a single strip into the paste. Pull the strip between 2 fingers in order to *remove as much excess paste as possible.* If the strips are too wet, the layers may come off and drying will take excessively long.

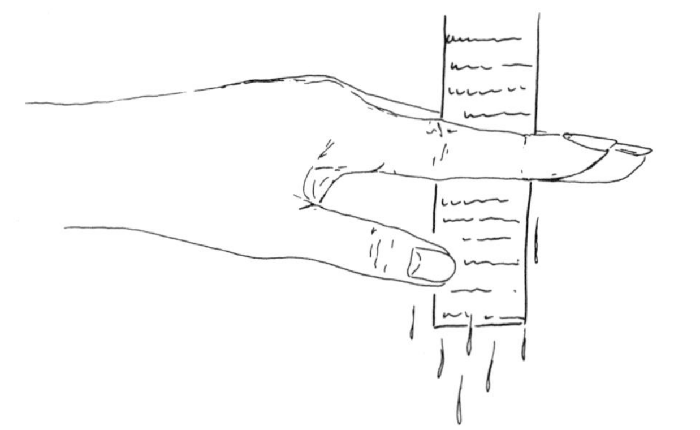

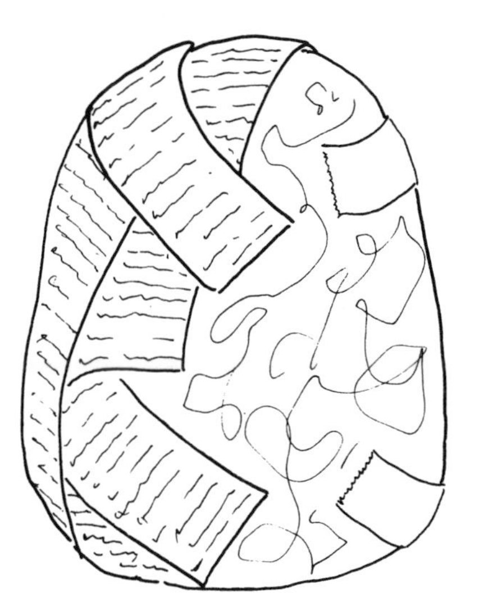

3) Apply one layer of strips to the form until it is completely covered. Each strip should overlap the previously applied strip by a small amount. Apply five (5) layers. It is very helpful, especially for children, to use the comic section of the newspaper (or any section with color) for every other layer in order to aid in remembering the number of layers applied. This can be done as follows:

1st layer	regular newspaper
2nd layer	comic section
3rd layer	regular newspaper
4th layer	comic section
5th layer	regular section

As the layers are applied, improve the shape by gently molding.

4) After the 5 layers have been applied, allow the papier-mâché to dry thoroughly. Drying can be accelerated by placing the form in the sun, near a heater, or in an oven at 350°F. To insure even and thorough drying, turn the form periodically.

5) When completely dry, cut a large flap at the base of the form and remove the crumpled newspaper and plastic bag.

6) Seal the flap with Scotch tape.

CRUMPLED NEWSPAPER

Step II: Application of the Plaster of Paris

Procedure:

1) Pour 125ml (1/2 cup) of water into the container and slowly sprinkle the plaster of Paris into the water. Continue adding the plaster until it forms a small mound above the surface of the water. Let the plaster soak up the water for about 2 minutes.

2) Using the plastic knife, spoon or your hand, stir slowly to keep the mixture moving. Air bubbles will rise to the surface. Gently tilt the container from time to time to allow more bubbles to rise. Remove any scum that may form on the surface (this is a sign of old plaster - if excessive amount forms, discard plaster).

3) Continue stirring until the mixture gets to a heavy cream consistency. It should have enough body to adhere. It is then ready for use.

4) Apply the plaster to the very bottom of the base of the form with a plastic knife or spoon. The plaster should be 3mm to 1.1cm (1/8" to 1/4") in thickness, or about the thickness of 3 dime coins. Smoothen the plaster so that it forms a rounded cap over the base of the form, tapering smoothly on the sides, as shown in the illustration. Since the plaster hardens in about 15 minutes, you must work quickly.

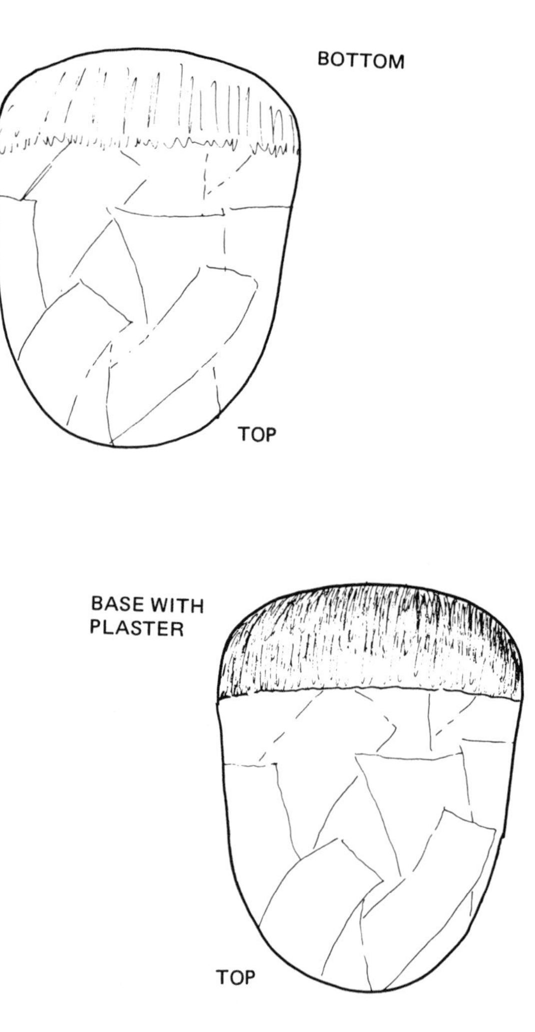

5) Prop the doll up to dry, with the plaster base upward. When dry, the base may be filed or sanded smooth.

Step III: Framing the Facial Features
(by making a ridge around the face area)

NOTE: This step will add character to the face, but *can be omitted* if short on time or if a simple, smooth-faced daruma is desired.

Procedure:

1) Using a piece of newspaper approximately 19cm by 30cm (7-1/2" by 12"), fold in half lengthwise, roll to about a No. 2 pencil size in circumference.

2) Tape the rolled newspaper onto the doll form to make a ridged outline of the face.

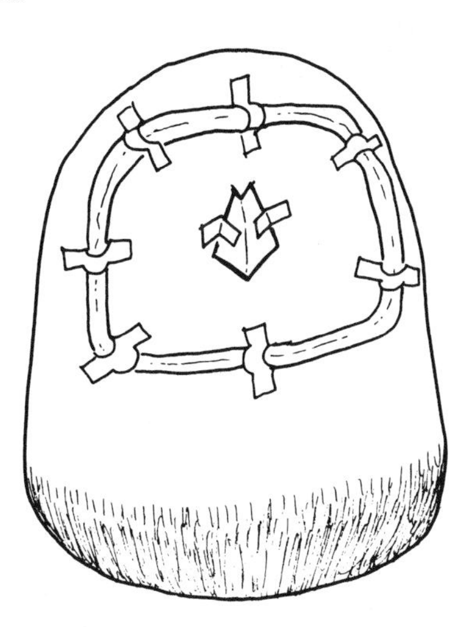

3) Using lightweight cardboard, index card or tagboard, create a shape for the nose. Tape the nose in place.

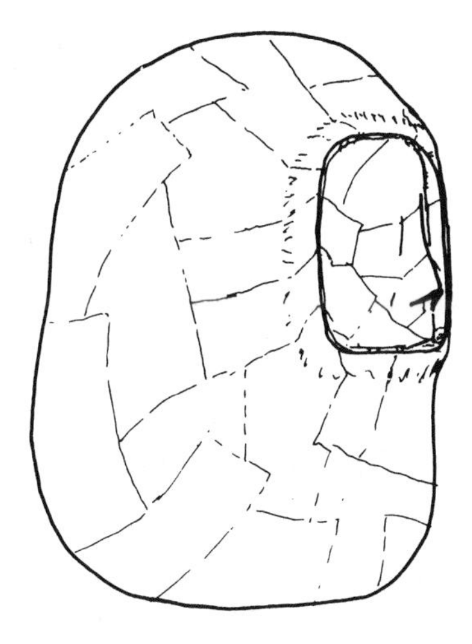

4) Cover the entire face area, ridge and nose, with 3 layers of newspaper strips which have been dipped in the wheat paste mixture (see Step I, under papier-mâché).

5) Let dry thoroughly.

Step IV: Painting

Procedure:

1) When thoroughly dry, paint the face area with flesh-colored paint and the rest of surface with red poster paint.

2) Paint on the facial features and add any other design you desire, using black, white, yellow, or any other colors.

3) For a high gloss finish, coat with lacquer or shellac.

OWAN

OZŌNI

(traditional soup with *mochi*)

5 servings

INGREDIENTS:

1 liter (4 C.) *dashi* (soup stock, recipe to follow) or clear broth

250 grams (1/2 lb.) boned chicken meat

1/3 of a block of *kamaboko* (steamed fish cake)

125ml (1/2 C.) sliced *takenoko* (bamboo shoots)

1 bunch of spinach (small young leaves)

10 *mochi* (pounded rice cakes)

Slice chicken thin and sprinkle lightly with salt. Cut fish cake lengthwise in half, and slice into 3mm (1/8") pieces. The bamboo shoots are cut diagonally across and then lengthwise into 3mm (1/8") slices. Wash spinach, cut off stems. Need about 2 to 3 leaves per soup serving.

Broil *mochi* to a "puffy" state, without browning. Heat *dashi*, add chicken slices, which will cook quickly. Add fish cake, bamboo shoots, and spinach to warm. Spinach should retain its green color.

Into each soup bowl, place 2 *mochi*, chicken slices, bamboo shoots, fish cake and spinach, and soup stock. Serve hot.

DASHI (soup stock) made from *katsuobushi* (dried bonito fillet) and *konbu* (dried kelp)

INGREDIENTS:

10 grams (about 1/3 oz.) *konbu*

10 grams (about 1/3 oz.) *katsuobushi*, freshly shaved or packaged shavings

1 liter (4 C.) water

Rinse kelp. Boil water in pot, and add kelp. Stir kelp several times, and remove from pot. Add shaved bonito to boiling water, and remove from flame immediately. Let stand for 1 minute. Strain and use clear liquid for soup stock.

OR, purchase *dashi no moto* (packaged, instant, soup stock) at a local Japanese food market and make broth as directed. Several brands are available.

Season *dashi* with 7 to 10ml (1-1/2 to 2 tsp.) salt, 15ml (1 T.) *shōyu* and a dash of sugar, or adjust seasoning to own taste.

Other ingredients can be put into the *ozōni*: fish meat, eggs, mushrooms, *tofu* (bean cake), shrimp, green onion. Lemon peel or ginger may be added for extra flavor.

OSECHI RYŌRI

(boiled vegetable; traditional dish for New Year)

serves 5 as main dish

INGREDIENTS:

1 liter (4 C.) *dashi* (clear soup stock) or clear chicken broth

shōyu (soy sauce)

sugar

salt

mirin (sweet rice wine for cooking)

10 *satoimo* (taro)

125 grams (1/4 lb.) string beans

2 carrots

1 small can *fuki* (coltsfoot), drained

2 large whole *takenoko* (bamboo shoot)

10 small dried *shiitake* (mushroom)

1-2 squares *konnyaku* (made from starch of a tuberous root of a plant called "devil's tongue")

2 *gobō* (burdock root)

GENERAL COOKING INSTRUCTIONS:

The vegetables are cooked separately and seasoned to bring out the natural flavor of each vegetable. The amount of soup stock or water used varies as to quantity of vegetable. Generally, enough liquid should be used so that during the cooking process, the boiling liquid will cover the vegetable. When liquid boils down, add more soup stock to maintain desired level.

SATOIMO:

Peel outer skin off with paring knife, and leave whole. Place into saucepan, cover with cold water and bring to a boil. Cook until slightly tender, drain. In another saucepan, bring to boil the following ingredients: 250ml (1 C.) *dashi*, 23ml (1-1/2 T.) sugar, 30ml (2 T. *shōyu*, 15ml (1 T.) *mirin*. Add hot *satoimo* into mixture and cook slowly until tender. Turn gently, periodically, to insure even coloring of *satoimo*. Remove cooked *satoimo*, and discard the liquid.

STRING BEANS:

Trim ends and string the beans. Place into boiling *dashi*, which has been seasoned with 15ml (1 T.) sugar and 5ml (1 tsp.) salt. Cook, uncovered, at a rapid boil until tender-crisp. The string beans will retain their fresh green color when cooked in this fashion. Take string beans out of cooking liquid, saving the liquid for the next vegetable.

CARROTS:

Cut into flower shapes by first making 4 "v" grooves down the length of carrot as illustrated. Cut the carrot into about 1.5cm (1/2") slices.

Into boiling seasoned *dashi* left from string beans, cook at rapid boil until carrots are tender-crisp. Remove carrots from liquid and save liquid for next vegetable.

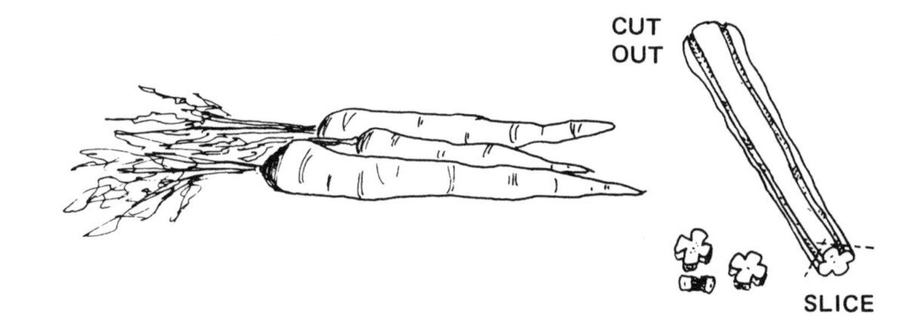

FUKI (coltsfoot):

Bring liquid to a boil. Add more *dashi* and sugar and salt, as needed. Add *fuki*, and heat vegetable thoroughly in boiling liquid. Remove from liquid.

TO THE LEFTOVER COOKING LIQUID, ADD: 45ml (3 T.) *shōyu*, 30ml (2 T.) *mirin*, 15ml (1 T.) sugar. The amount of liquid should be about 500ml (2 cups). Add broth as needed to cover vegetables as they cook.

TAKENOKO:

Cut into diagonal chunks about the same size as the *satoimo*. Cut as illustrated:

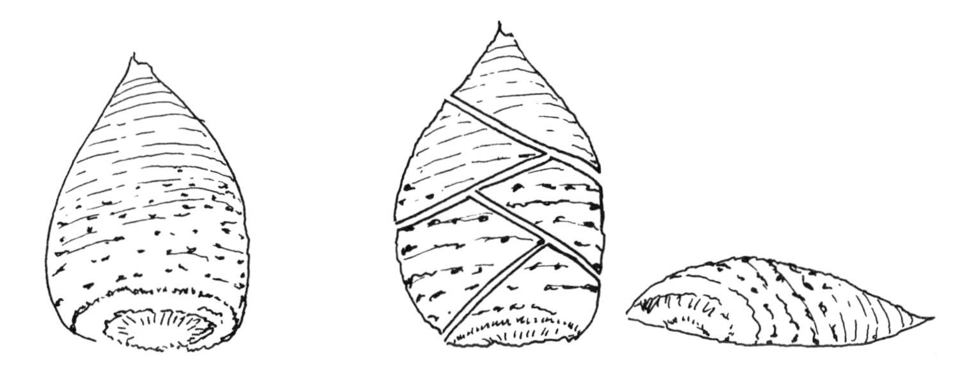

Add bamboo shoots to boiling seasoned broth, turn gently periodically to insure even coloring and cook until tender. Remove from liquid, which is saved.

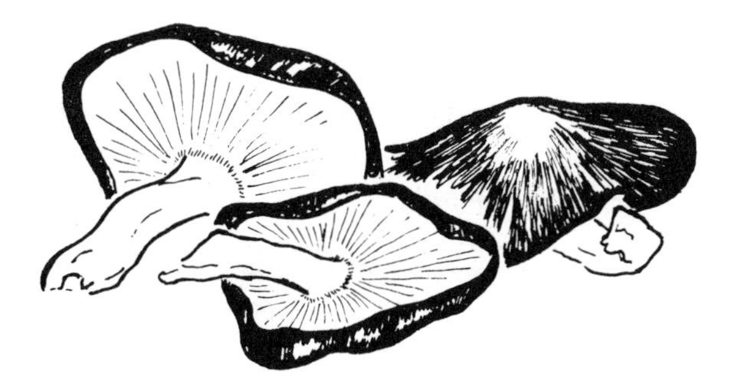

SHIITAKE:

Remove mushrooms, which have been soaking in cold water, and discard the hard stems. Add mushrooms to boiling liquid and cook until tender. Remove from cooking liquid.

GOBŌ:

Wash root with scrub brush, or scrape outer skin off with paring knife. Cut into 2.5cm (2") lengths, angling ends as illustrated:

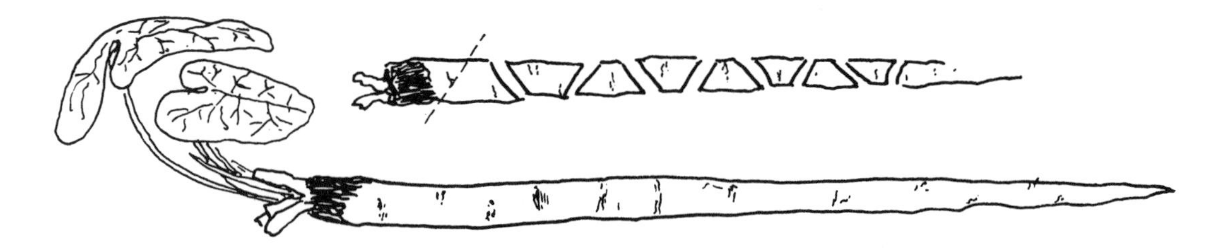

Cook in rapid boiling liquid until tender. Remove from liquid.

KONNYAKU:

Cut into bite-size triangles. Cook in rapid boiling liquid until tender. Remove from liquid.

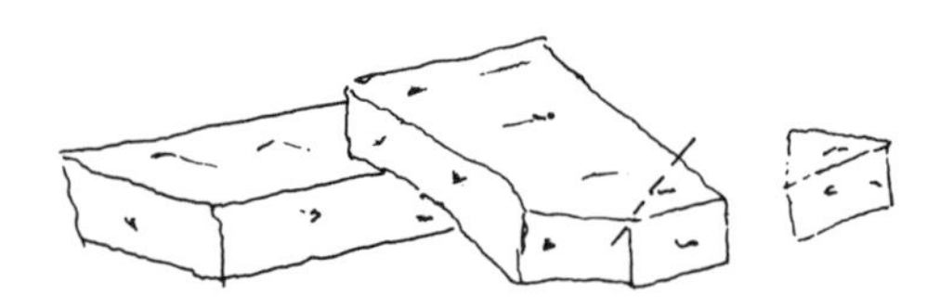

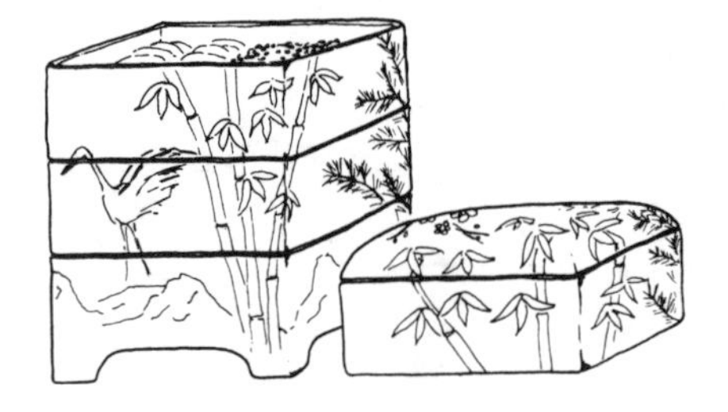

With all the vegetables cooked, gently mix together in serving bowl. *Teriyaki* (soy sauce and sugar marinade) chicken in bite-size pieces can be served alongside, or mixed with the boiled vegetables. With the chicken, this dish is called *umani*. Both *osechi ryōri* and *umani* are served cold, at room temperature.

KUCHITORI (side dishes): There are endless varieties of side dishes. The two given here are probably the most common.

KANTEN (Agar Agar):

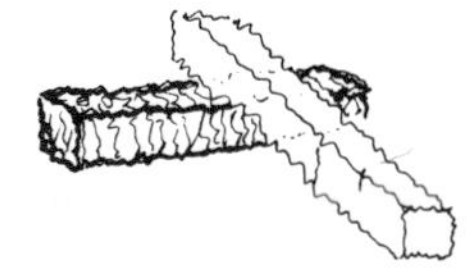

INGREDIENTS:

2 sticks of *kanten* (Agar Agar), comes clear or red colored

1 liter (4 C.) water

250ml (1 C.) sugar

pinch of salt

2-3 drops of vanilla, cinnamon, and/or lemon extract

If you are going to make both red and clear (white) *kanten*, make the clear batch first. The red color affects utensils, etc. used in cooking and will tint the clear *kanten*.

Wash the sticks of *kanten*. Squeeze out water, and shred the sticks into a large pot. Add water, and soak for half an hour. Cook over medium heat until *kanten* is dissolved. Add sugar, salt and continue to cook until sugar is dissolved. Remove from heat, add flavoring. Strain liquid into a 20.3 x 20.3cm (8" x 8") pan. Place in refrigerator or cool place to harden. Cut into oblong strips, triangles, or any shape desired.

KUROMANE (black beans):

An old world recipe suggested that an old iron nail be placed in the cooking beans to insure softness. It has not been tried out, and we do not recommend this method.

INGREDIENTS:

500 grams (1 lb.) *kuromane* (black beans)

250ml (1 C.) sugar, or sweeten to taste

(about) 63ml (1/4 C.) salted soft *konbu* (kelp)

Wash and soak beans overnight. Cook in 1 liter (4 cups) of water until beans are soft. Add water as necessary to maintain a water level of 2.5cm (1") above the beans until the beans begin to soften. Add sugar and *konbu*, cook for another 1/2 hour. Sugar will harden the beans, so be sure that the beans are soft before adding sugar. For variation, add boiled, peeled chestnuts with the sugar and *konbu*.

SUNOMONO (vinegared dish): All sorts of combinations of fresh vegetables, cooked shellfish can be created into *sunomono*. The important part is the *sanbaizu* (vinegar sauce).

SANBAIZU:

INGREDIENTS:

250ml (1 C.) rice vinegar

200 to 250ml (3/4 to 1 C.) sugar

5ml (1 tsp.) salt

15ml (1 T.) *shōyu* (soy sauce)

Combine ingredients and boil to dissolve the sugar. Cool before using. May be stored for later use.

RENKON NO SUNOMONO
(vinegared lotus root):

INGREDIENTS:

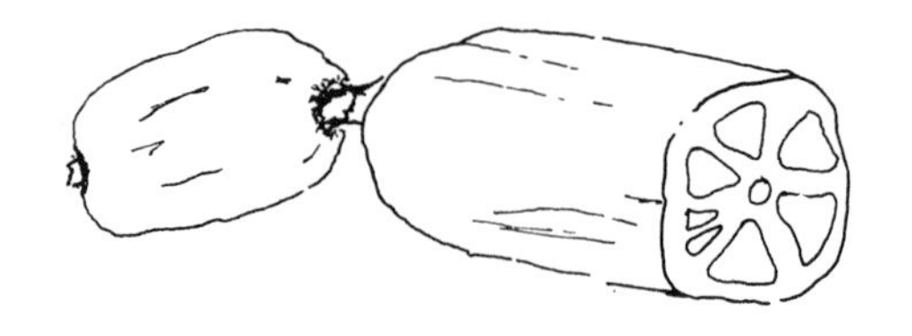

2 *renkon* (lotus root)

15ml (1 T.) white vinegar

Salt

Wash and peel outer skin. Boil whole *renkon* in water with vinegar and a dash of salt, for about 5 minutes. Slice *renkon*, crosswise, about 2 to 3mm (1/8") thickness. Cook in *sanbaizu* for about 4 minutes. *Renkon* should be *shari-shari* (crunchy).

雛祭

HINAMATSURI (Doll Display)

BONBORI

MOMO-NO HANA

BYŌBU

TONO-SAMA

OHIME-SAMA

SANBŌ

DAIRI-SAMA

KAGAMI
MOCHI

SAGE
CHŌSHI

SAKAZUKI

SANBŌ

NAGAE
CHŌSHI

KANJO

TAIKO

ŌKAWA

KOTSUTSUMI

FUE

UTAI

GONIN BAYASHI

UKON-E

SAKON-E

HISHIMOCHI

YADAIJIN

TACHIBANA

SAKURA

TATEZASA
WARAI
JŌGO

KUTSUDAI
NAKI
JŌGO

DAIZASA
OKORI
JŌGO

JICHŌ

HINAMATSURI

*Hinamatsuri** (Dolls' Festival or Girls' Day) is celebrated yearly on March 3rd, by Japanese families with daughters. Special dolls are brought out and displayed on this day.

During the weeks prior to *Hinamatsuri*, department stores all over Japan sell huge selections of *Hinamatsuri* sets in all sizes and styles. School and public offices, as well as places of business, display the doll sets, and confectionery shops and bakeries make sweets and cakes for the occasion.

Traditionally, we picture girls in *kimono* serving *ochagashi* (small tea cakes), *amazake* or *shirozake* (thick, sweet, white rice wine) and *sekihan* (rice cooked with red *azuki* beans) to their family and friends in honor of the displayed dolls. Although these traditions still exist, many girls simply enjoy the displaying of these dolls without the formalities, just for the pleasure of having them. Japanese generally regard dolls as symbolic ornaments rather than playthings.

In the United States, many Japanese American girls also take pleasure in displaying *Hinamatsuri* dolls. But, as might be expected, many differences occur not only in the attitudes and feelings about the dolls, but also in what is displayed and in the activities related to the display. The American style may incorporate regular, common American dolls with the traditional Japanese ones.

The styles and types of *Hinamatsuri* dolls are numerous. They appear as both adults and children, and are usually made of porcelain and cloth, sometimes of paper or carved from wood. Commonly fifteen dolls are displayed as a set placed on the *hinadan* (a step-like structure) with 5 to 7 tiers and covered with a bright red cloth. The red symbolizes the color of the sun, vigor and good fortune.

The main dolls are usually called *Dairi-sama*** (Court people). This pair (male and female dolls) alone would be sufficient for a *Hinamatsuri* display.

The male doll is referred to as *Taishi-sama* (the Imperial Prince) or more commonly *Tono-sama* (the feudal Lord); and, the female doll, *Ohime-sama* (Princess or Lady). Oftentimes these two dolls are thought of as the Emperor and Empress, in which case, they would be called *Tenno-sama* (Emperor) and *Kōgō-sama* (Empress). However, during the period when this festival was formulating, the Japanese venerated the Emperor and Empress so that to create dolls in their image would have been considered unpardonably rude and out of the question.

*This festival is sometimes called *Momo No Sekku* (Peach Blossom Festival).

***Dairi* means court and *sama* is a highly formal honorific title, much more formal than the title ending "san", i.e. Mr., Mrs., Miss, Ms).

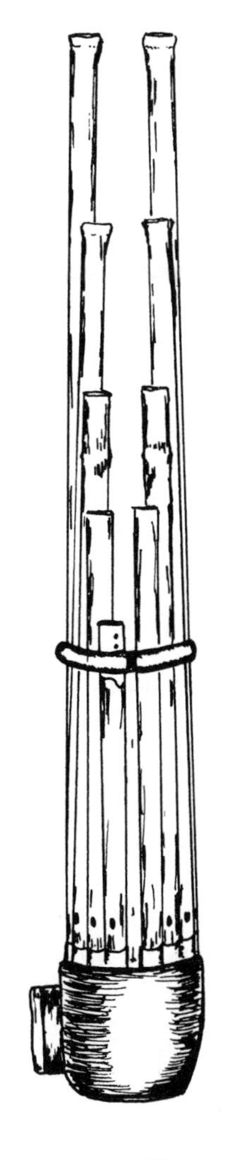

SHŌ　　HICHIRIKI　　ŌTEKI

The *Dairi-sama* are placed on the top shelf with the *Tono-sama* on the left and *Ohime-sama* on the right, as one faces the *hinadan*. Behind each of the dolls is a miniature *byōbu* (folding screen) serving as a background. *Bonbori* (lanterns) stand on both sides of the *Dairi-sama*. Between the *Tono-sama* and *Ohime-sama* is a *sanbō* (tray stand) with two *omikidokkuri* (ritual *sake* bottles) in which are branches of *sakaki* (sacred tree in Shintoism) or branches of *momo* (peach blossom, which symbolizes progeny, fertility and the reawakening of nature through Spring).

On the second tier down are three *Kanjo* (Ladies in Waiting) who represent three stages in life: youth, middle age, old age. They are serving *sake*. The Lady holding a *sakazuki* (lacquered *sake* cup) on a *sanbō* is in the middle. The Lady holding a *sage-chōshi* (pitcher or short *sake* server) is on the left, while one holding a *nagae-chōshi* (long handled *sake* server) is on the right. The serving of *sake* is important since *sake* is believed to be an elixir of life. On this tier also are placed two tall stemmed stands to hold *kagami mochi* (pounded rice cakes) as offerings to the *Dairi-sama*.

Five Court Musicians occupy the third tier. If these dolls have child-like features, they are called *Gonin Bayashi* and are placed in this order: (left to right) *taiko* (drum), *ōkawa* (lap drum), *kotsutsumi* (shoulder drum), *fue* (flute), and *utai* (singer). If the dolls have adult-like features, they are called *Gagaku Reijin* and placed in this order: (left to right) *shoko* (gong), *kaen taiko* (large standing drum), *shō* (18-pipe mouth organ), *hichiriki* (type of oboe), and *ōteki* (flute).

On the fourth tier stand two *Yadaijin* (Ministers). The old man on the right is *Sakon-e*, Protector of the Left (side), and the young man on the left is *Ukon-e*, Protector of the Right. Although collectively the pair is called *Yadaijin*, it is by title only and their function is that of guards, rather than statesmen.

The lacquered trays holding *hishimochi* (tri-colored *mochi* are placed between the *Yadaijin*. The diamond form of the *hishimochi* derives from the shape of the leaf of the *hishi* plant (water caltrop), which was thought to have medicinal properties of longevity. The three layers of color represent red for vigor, white for purity and green for fertility. Miniature dishes for the *Dairi-sama* are also placed on this tier.

Three *Jichō* (footmen) occupy the fifth tier. These three are also called *Sannin Jōgo* (three drunks, tipplers) because each face reflects the moods stimulated by drinking. The *Jichō* with the laughing face is *Warai Jōgo* (laughing drunk). He carries a *tatezasa* (long handled parade umbrella) and sits on the left side. The middle *Jichō* is *Naki Jōgo* (crying drunk) and holds the *kutsudai* (lacquered shoes on a platform), while the *Jichō* on the right is *Okori Jōgo* (mad/angry drunk), holding a *daizasa* (large umbrella). A *tachibana* (type of orange tree) is placed at the extreme left of this tier and a *sakura* (cherry blossom tree) is to the right.

The remaining lower tiers are for *dōgu* (tiny household utensils and articles), *naka-mochi* (chests and trunks), *hasami bako* (sewing stand), *gosho-guruma* (ox carriage) and *okago* (palanquin), which belong to the *Dairi-sama*.

Modern day *Hinamatsuri* arose as a mixture of various rituals and celebrations. During the Heian Era (794-1192), literary works* referred to *hina asobi* (small replica play = dolls with household appliances), that is, everyday play. Also at that time there were two celebrations which may have contributed to the development of *Hina-matsuri*: (1) *Kyokusui no en (kyoku* = music — *sui* = water — *en* = banquet), and (2) *Ono-miyoshi no harai no shiki* (*Onomiyoshi* = name of priest/teacher — *harai* = purification — *shiki* = ceremony). Both of these celebrations were held on the third day of the third lunar month.

Kyokusui no en started about 1,500 years ago during the era of Emperor Kenso. During the early part of the third day, the Emperor's household and noble guests would go to a nearby stream. The guests would seat themselves in various locations along the banks of the winding stream. From the head of the stream, *sakazuki* (wooden lacquered *sake* cups) were set adrift. By the time a floating *sakazuki* reaches a nobleman, he must have composed a *shiika* (special poem). If he has done so, he picks up the *sakazuki*, pours *sake* into it and drinks it. He then goes to a designated site, usually a palace, for a banquet at which he and the others would read their poems.

The special purification ritual associated with the third day of the third lunar month was called *Onomiyoshi no harai no shiki*. As part of this ceremony, *harai no kamihina* (purification paper replica/dolls) were fashioned, onto which people projected their unhappiness and ills. These paper dolls were then thrown into the river to carry away the ailments. The *harai no kamihina* gave rise to a charm replica called *amagatsu*, a doll made from two pieces of bamboo or wood, crossed in the middle, with a head and body of cloth or paper that was covered with an outside garment, the *kimono*. Sutra** verses were written on paper and secured to the mid-section of the doll.

Amagatsu is the personification of a baby, and such dolls were placed near the bedding of children to ward off evil. Boys would give up this charm at age 15 when they were considered to enter manhood, but girls kept the *amagatsu* until the time of their marriage when another doll charm, *oto-gibōko*, would take its place. *Otogibōko* was made from white fabric, filled with cotton, and had facial features as well as hair on the head. The combination of *amagatsu* and

*The literary works include *Tales of Genji* by Murasaki Shikibu and *The Pillow Book* by Sei Shōnagon.

**Sutra is a Sanskrit word literally meaning a classical text handed down from ancient times. In Japanese culture, sutra specifically refers to Buddhist texts.

otogibōko evolved into the *meoto ningyō* (a male and female pair of dolls). When you see this pair, the *o-hina* (male doll) has its sleeve spread out, standing upright, wearing a *hakama* (pant-skirt), and the *me-hina* (female doll) has the sleeves folded in front, standing upright, and wearing an *obi* (sash). These doll charms are classified collectively as *tachibina* (standing dolls) and, along with the *kamihina* (paper replica/dolls), are considered *kanhina* (god replica/dolls).

It is believed that the present dolls displayed at *Hinamatsuri* evolved from the combination of the *kanhina* and the *suwari-bina* (sitting replica). The *suwaribina* is bag-like with *kimono* garments draped over its cone-shaped body. It has a round knob head with painted line features. This type of *hina* seems to be the forerunner of the shape of the *Dairi-sama*.

MEOTO NINGYŌ

During the 6th year of the Kanei Era (1624-1643), Emperor Gomizuno-o's daughter, Princess Okiko, became Empress Meishō on her 7th birthday. Her mother, Tofukumon-in-sama, celebrated the occasion by displaying the dolls for her daughter in their Kyoto palace. Gradually, wealthy and high ranking families adopted this tradition. During the Genroku Era (1688-1703), a cultural revolution refined the craft of making *Dairi-sama* and other dolls were added to the display.

By 1770, *Hinamatsuri* became a national holiday in Japan and remained so until the 6th year of the Meiji Reformation (1874) when the holiday status of the festival was removed. Over the years this custom has gradually regained popularity, but this time not only among nobility, but also among Japanese in general. Today, although it is not an official holiday, practically everyone in Japan celebrates this happy festival.

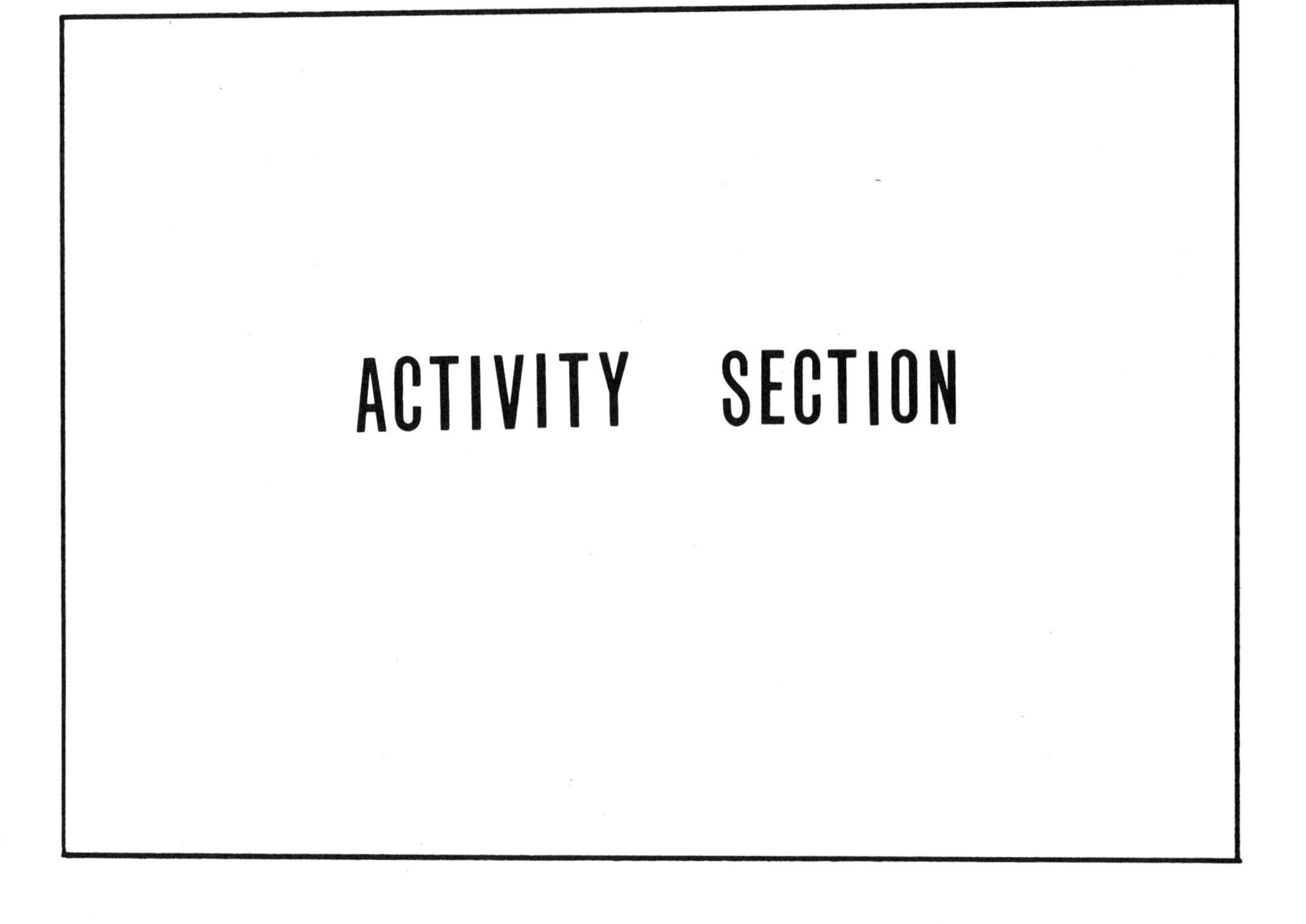
ACTIVITY SECTION

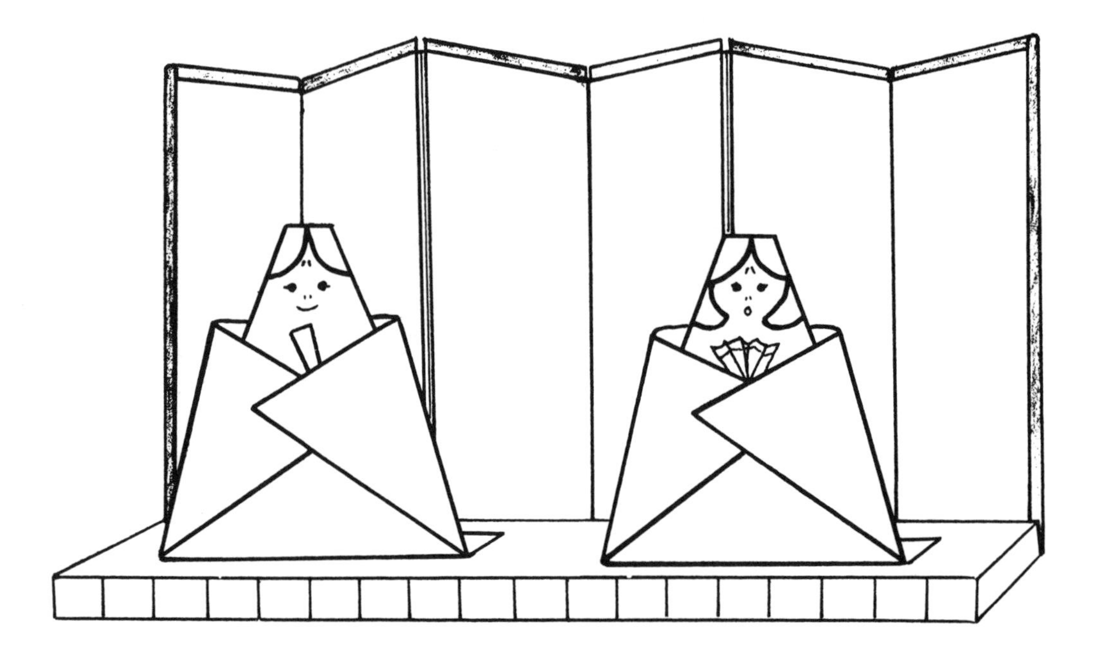

DAIRI-SAMA (Origami)

HINAMATSURI

A simple, inexpensive *Hinamatsuri* (Girls' Day) doll set can be made by *origami* (paper folding). Instructions are given here for making 15 paper dolls. Also, instructions for making a *sanbō* (tray) out of paper are given. Paper *sanbō* can be used as a container for candy, nuts, or anything else.

MATERIALS:

- *Origami* paper, or any paper cut into squares (fadeless colored paper, gift wrapping paper). Avoid thick or very thin paper, because it will be difficult to make folds.
- Pencil and coloring materials (felt-tip pens, colored pencils, crayons)
- White glue and scotch tape
- Scissors
- Backboard (heavy cardboard, bulletin board, etc.) or blocks of wood
- Red paper or cloth to cover the backboard.

GENERAL INSTRUCTIONS:

All 15 dolls are made using the basic ORIGAMI DOLL pattern. All the dolls are made from one square sheet of paper, the same size, with the exception of the Standing (middle) *Kanjo* and the *Yadaijin* (Ministers), which require two sheets of paper the same size.

The facial features can be drawn directly onto the folded figures, or drawn separately, cut out, and pasted to the figures. Patterns for faces and paraphernalia are given.

Other accessories, such as the screen, lantern stands, trays, trees, can be made from paper cut-outs and added to the set. (See illustrations for ideas.)

The finished set can be attached to a backboard covered with red paper, or displayed on blocks covered with red cloth or paper, stacked in a stair-like fashion. If the display is to be attached to a backboard, that is flat, omit Step 6 of the folding instructions.

ORIGAMI DOLL

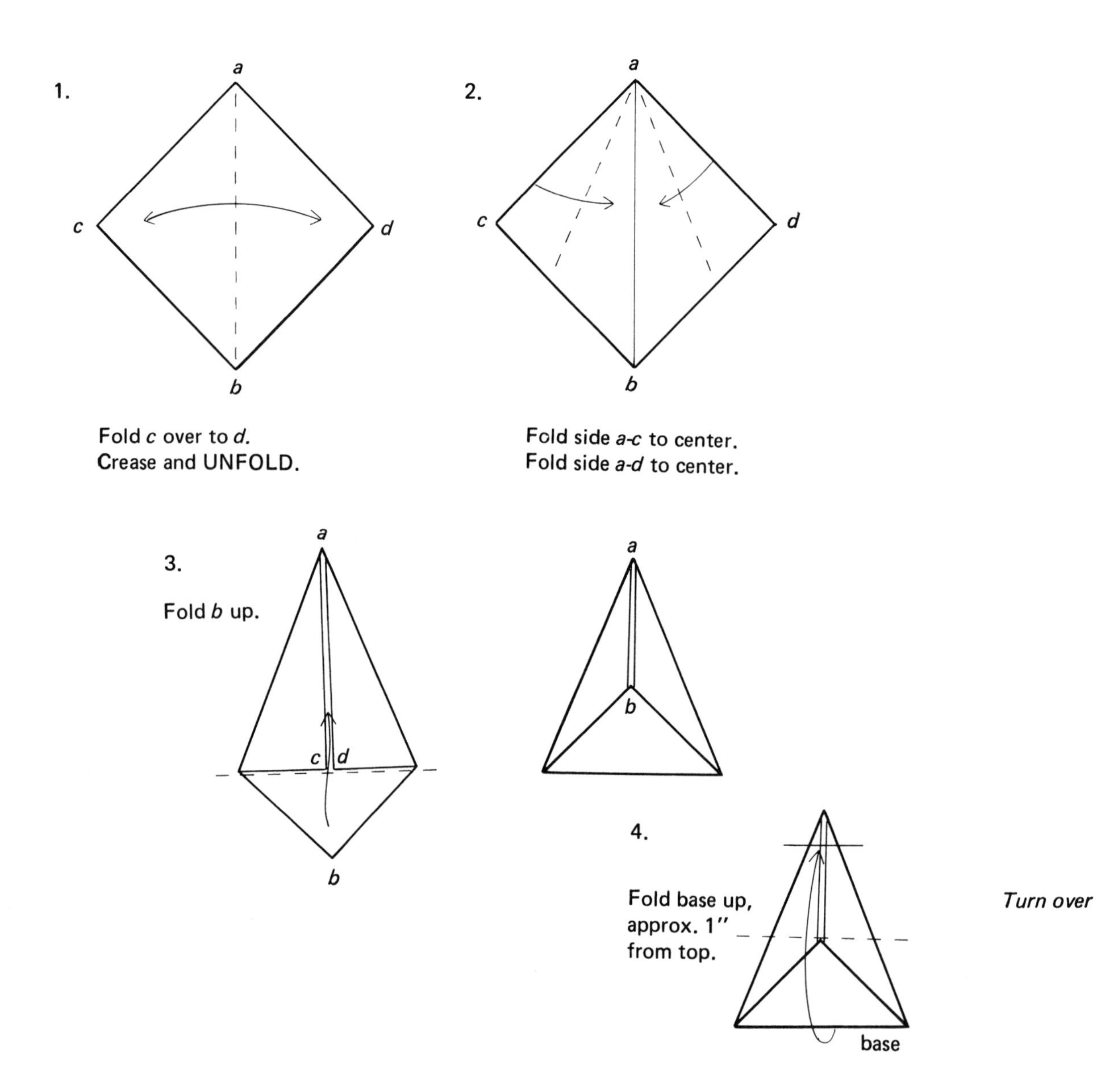

5.

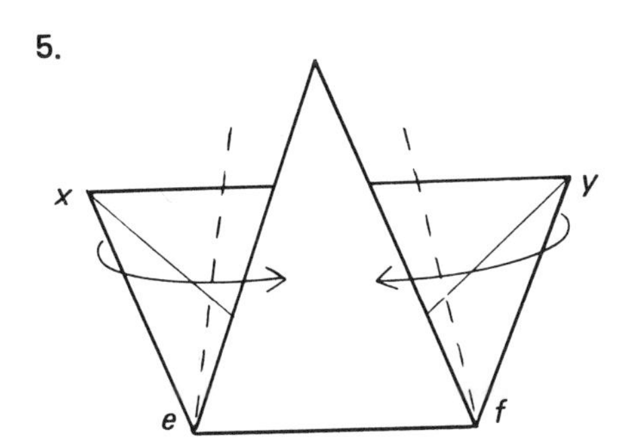

Fold sides *x-e* and *y-f* to center. *x-e* should be under *y-f* . These form the "sleeves".

6.

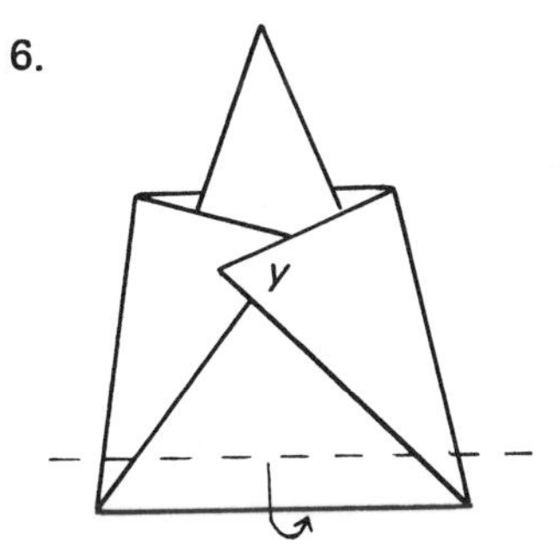

Fold base back to make doll sit upright.

7.

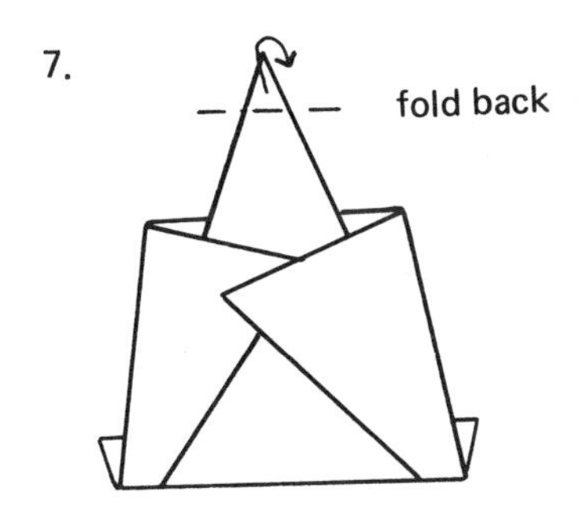

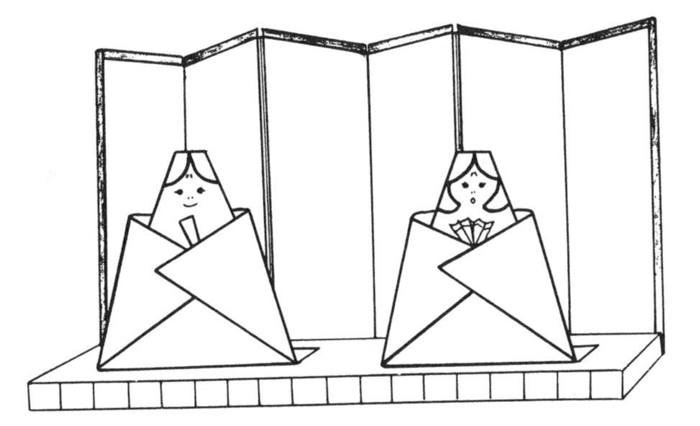

STANDING (middle) KANJO

1) Make the "ORIGAMI DOLL" for top section.

2) To make bottom section:
   1 – 3: Start with steps 1-3 of "ORIGAMI DOLL".

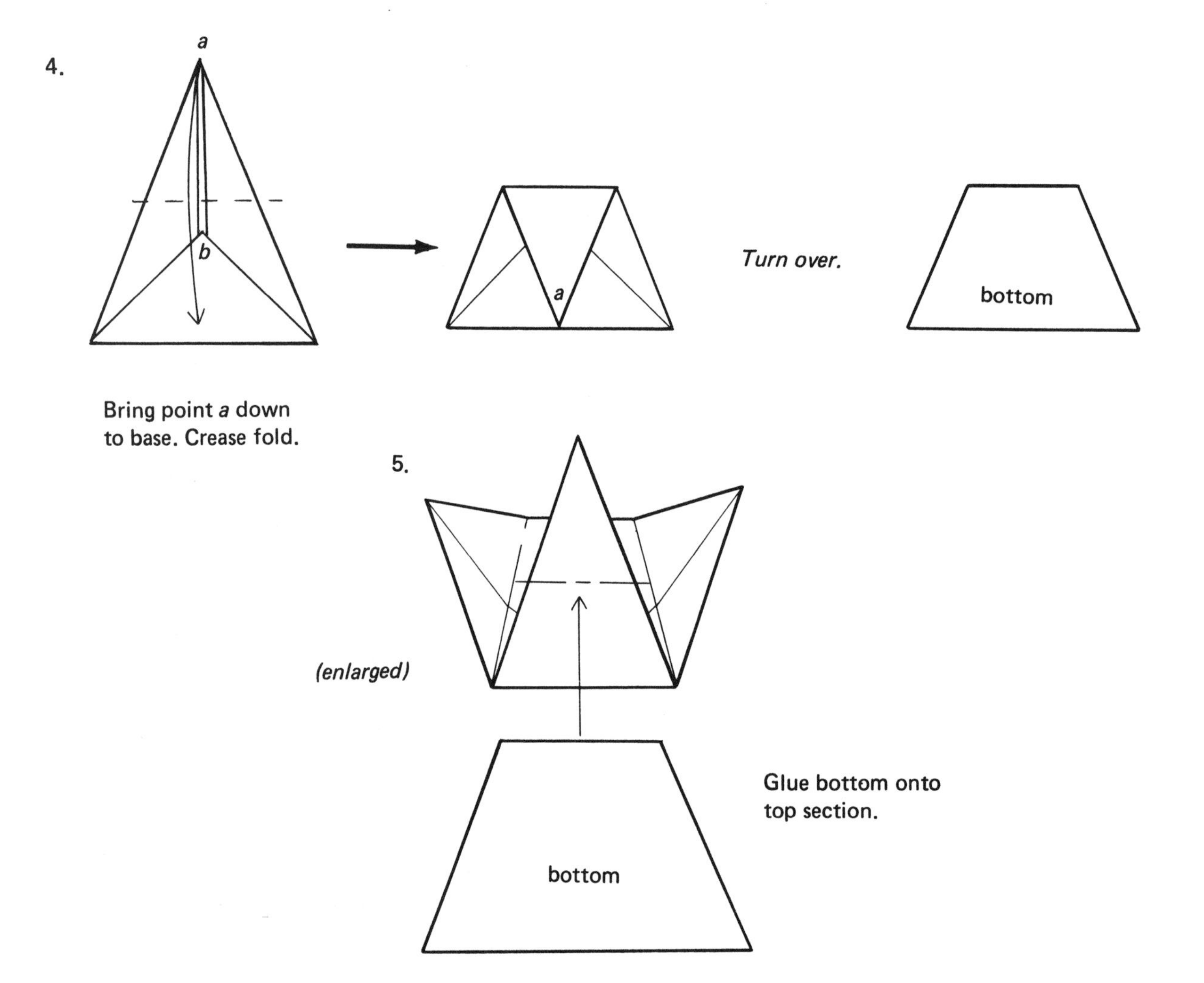

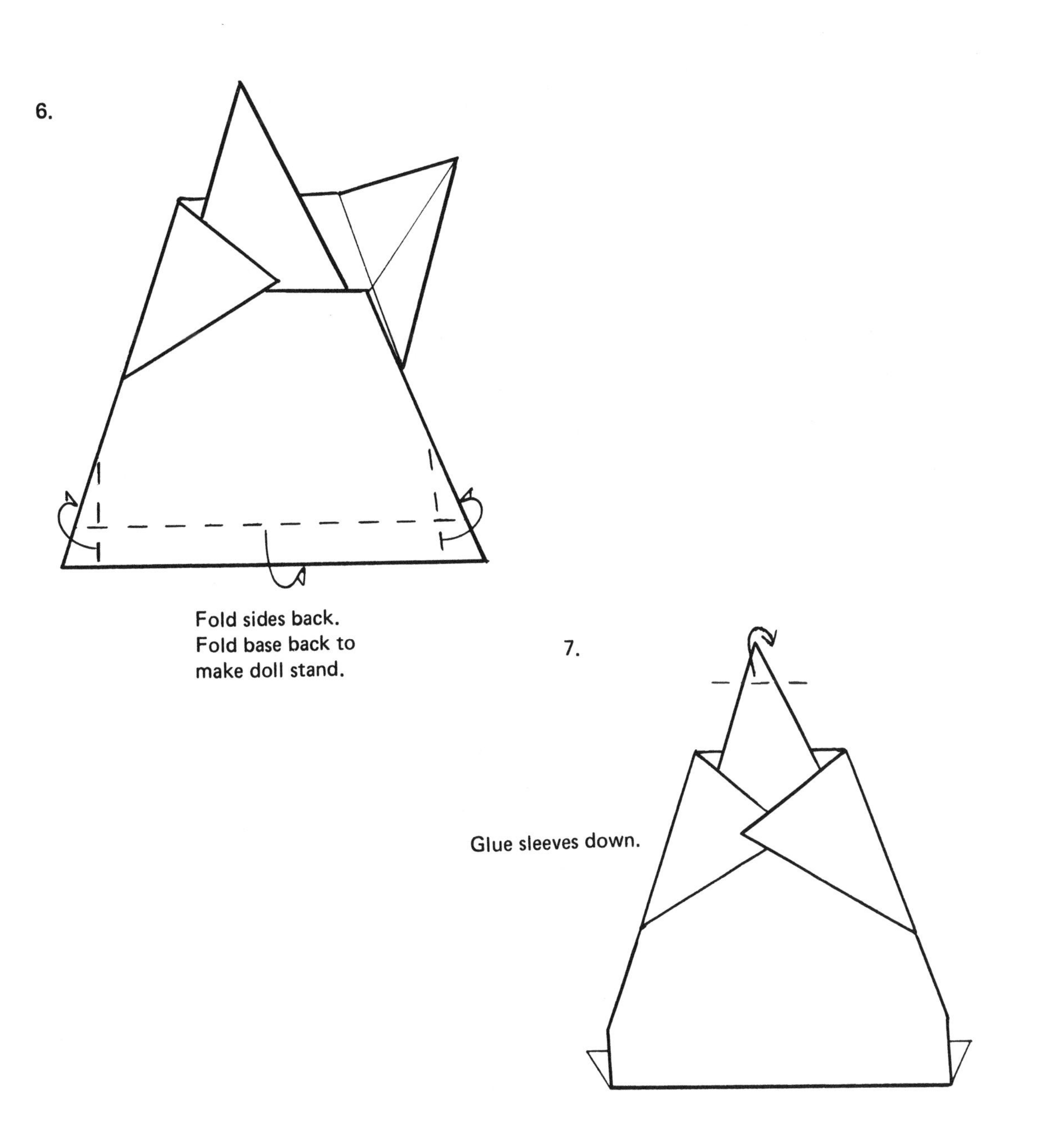
6.
Fold sides back.
Fold base back to
make doll stand.
7.
Glue sleeves down.

YADAIJIN (ministers)

HAKAMA (pant-skirt)

To make the YADAIJIN:

1) Make the "ORIGAMI DOLL" for top section

2) To make HAKAMA: 1 – 3

Start with steps 1-3 of "ORIGAMI DOLL".

4.

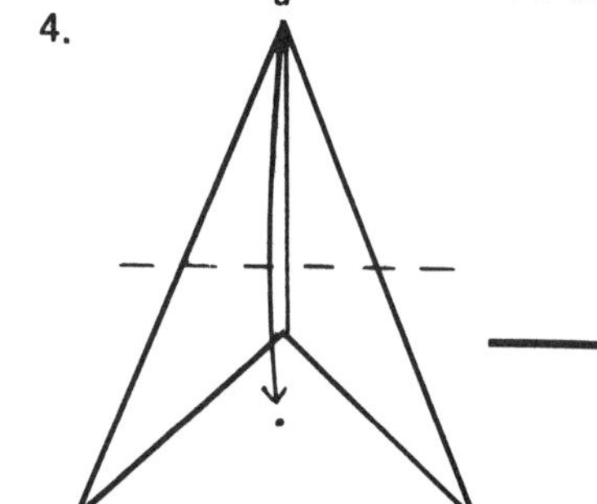

Bring point *a* down to dot.

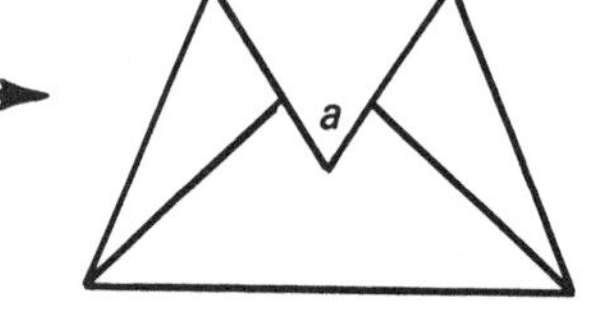

Turn over.

5.

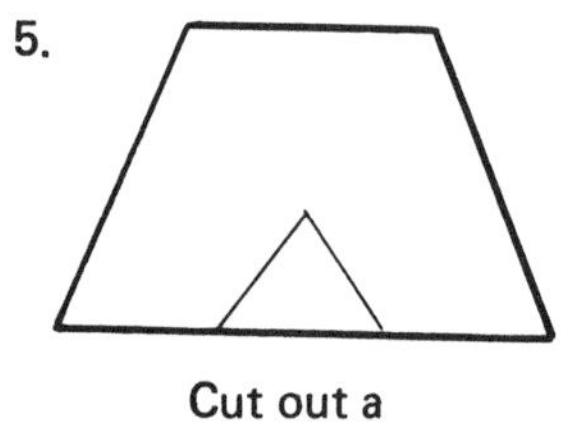

Cut out a triangular piece at base.

6.

Fold base back.

7.

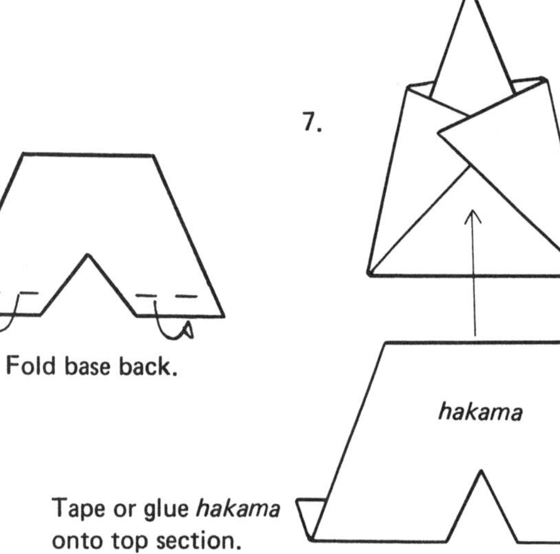

Tape or glue *hakama* onto top section.

8.

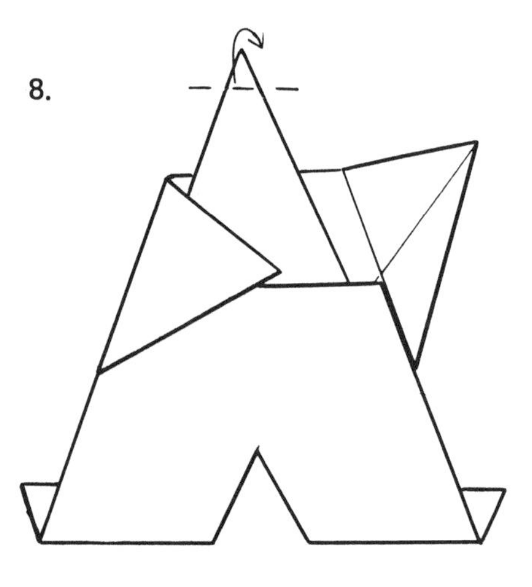

DAIRI SAMA

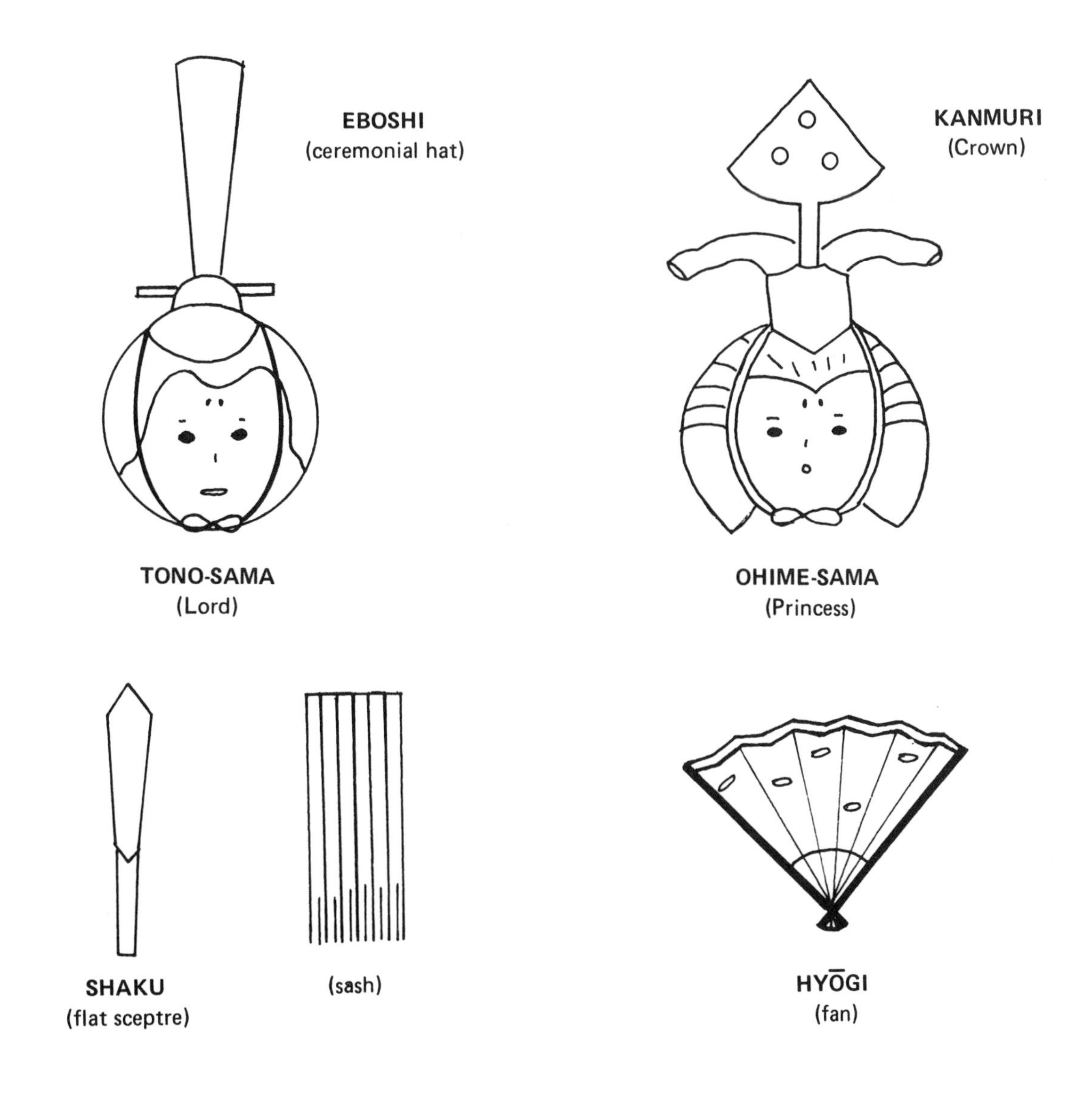
EBOSHI
(ceremonial hat)
KANMURI
(Crown)
TONO-SAMA
(Lord)
OHIME-SAMA
(Princess)
SHAKU
(flat sceptre)
(sash)
HYŌGI
(fan)

KANJO
(Ladies-in-Waiting)

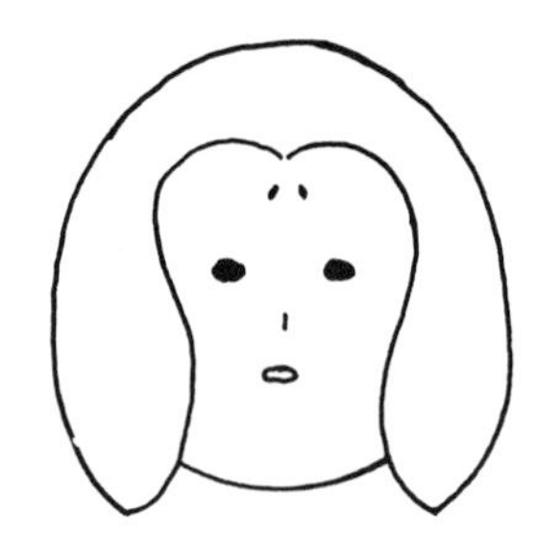

SAGE-CHŌSHI (*sake* server)

SAKAZUKI
(lacquered *sake* cups)

SANBŌ
(lacquered stand)

NAGAE-CHŌSHI
(long handled *sake* server)

GONIN BAYASHI
(5 musicians)

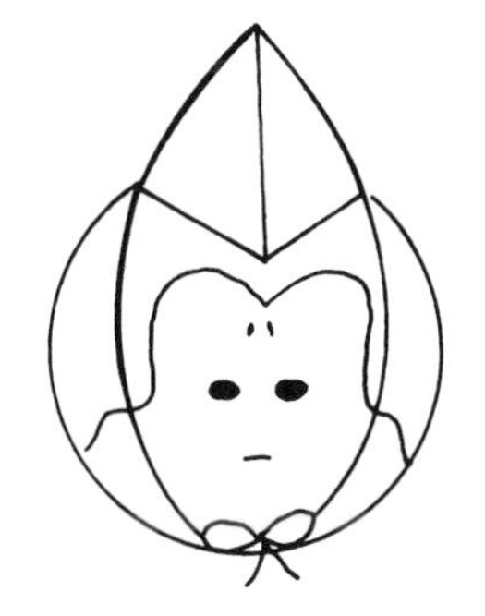

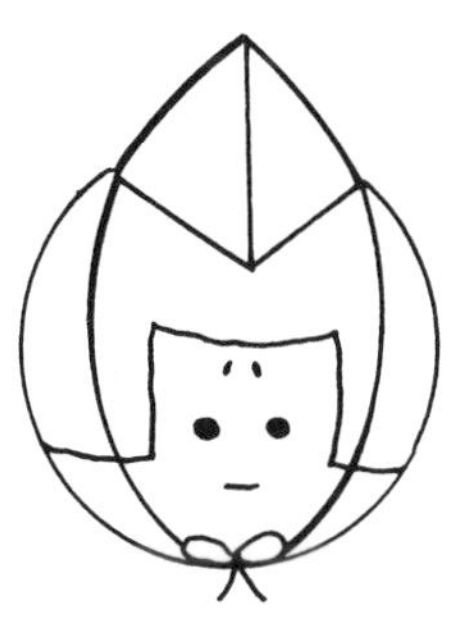

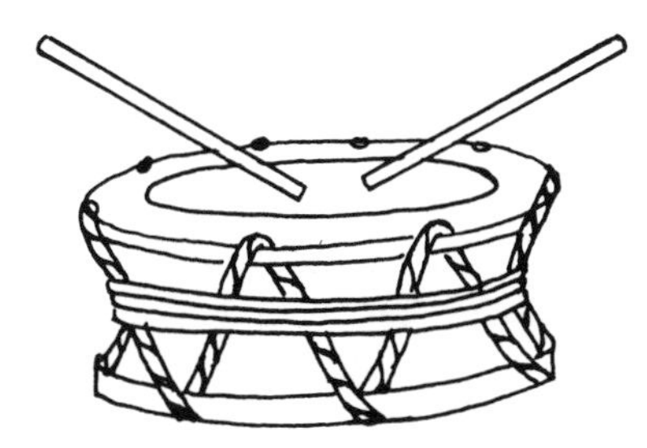

TAIKO
(drum)

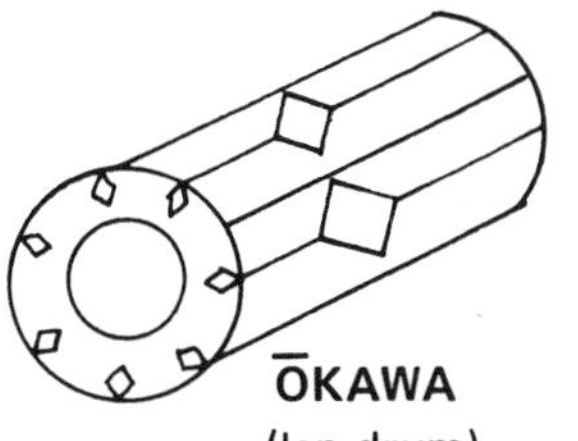

ŌKAWA

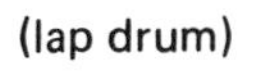

(lap drum)

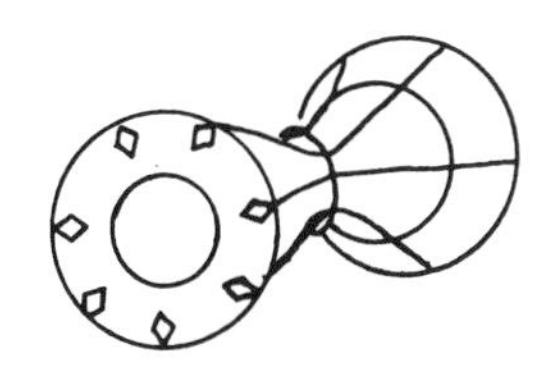

KOTSUTSUMI
(shoulder drum)

FUE
(flute)

SENSU
(fan)

UTAI
(singer)

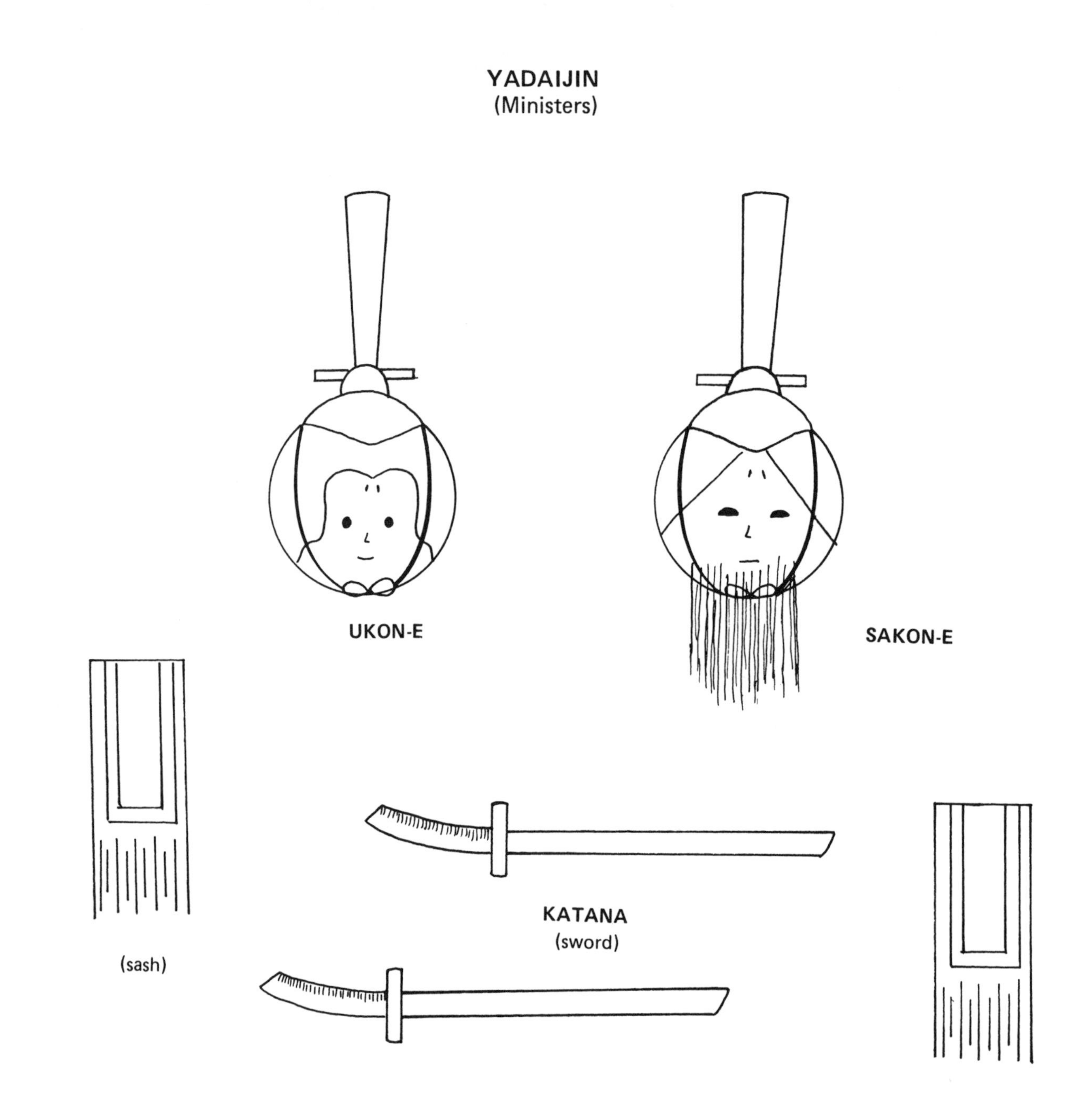
YADAIJIN
(Ministers)
UKON-E
SAKON-E
KATANA
(sword)
(sash)

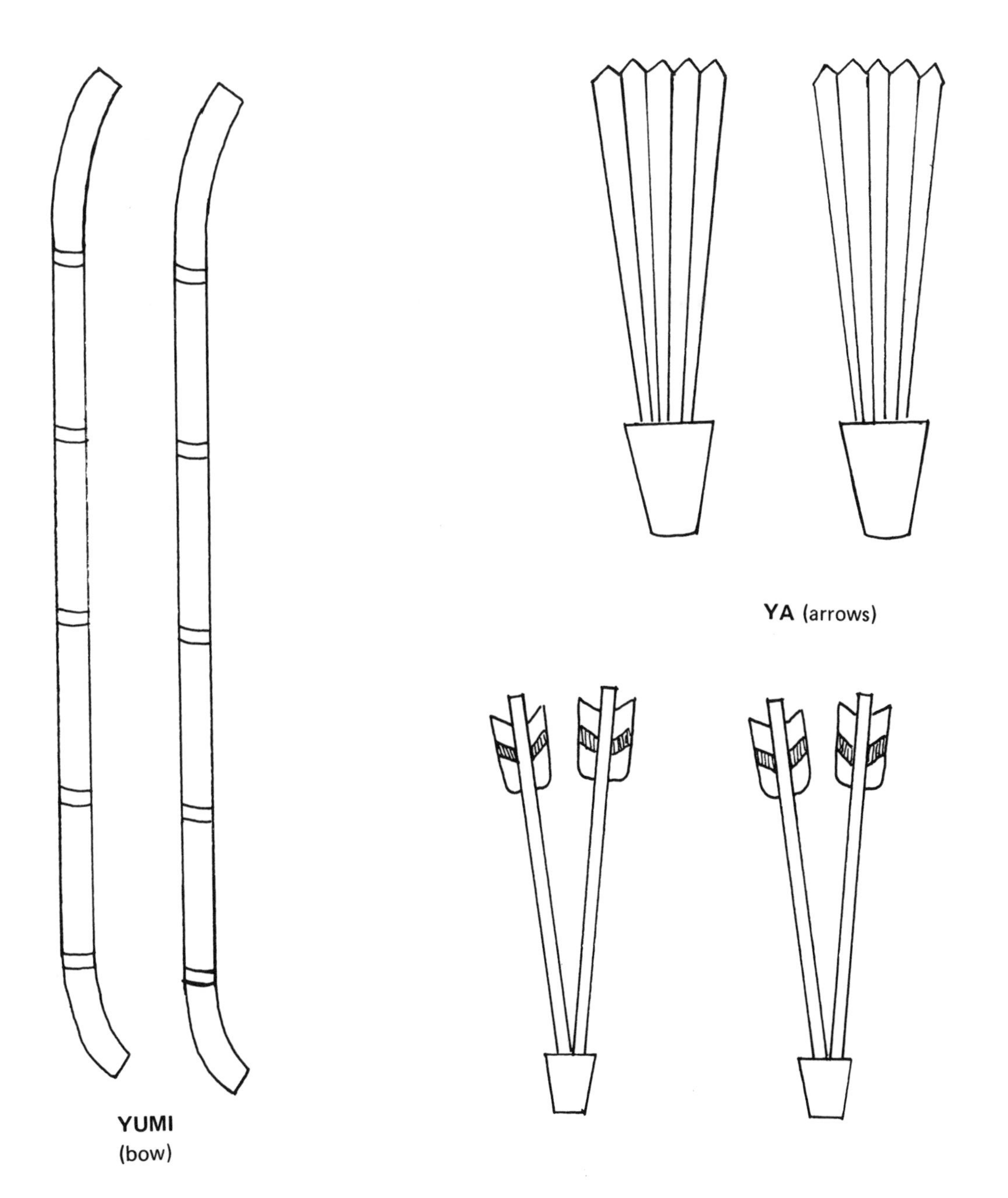
YA (arrows)
YUMI
(bow)

JICHŌ
(footmen)

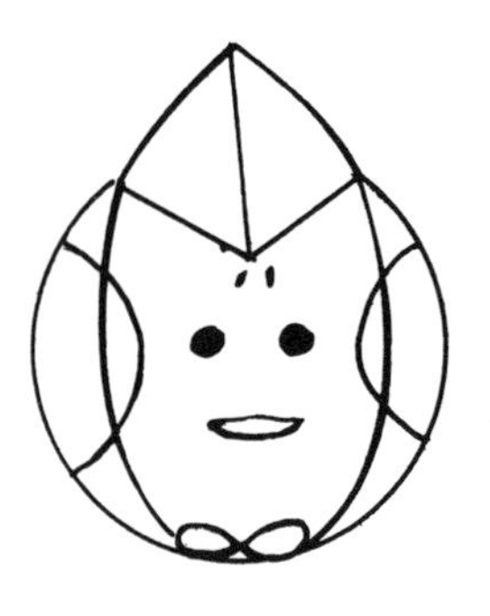

WARAI JŌGO

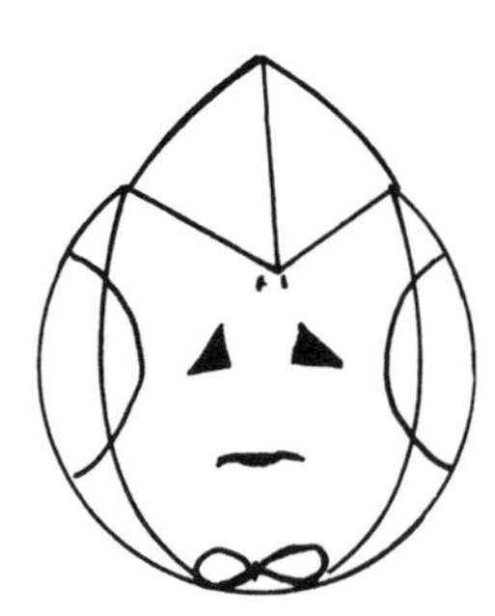

NAKI JŌGO

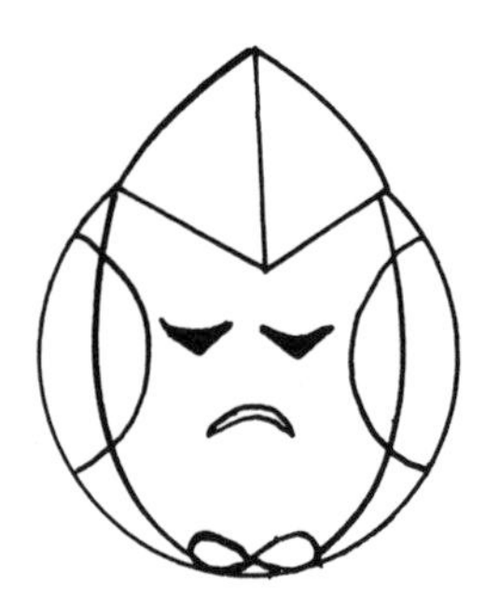

OKORI JŌGO

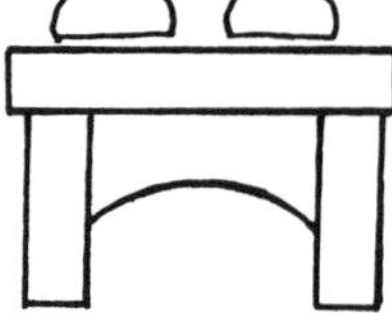

KUTSUDAI
(lacquered shoes)

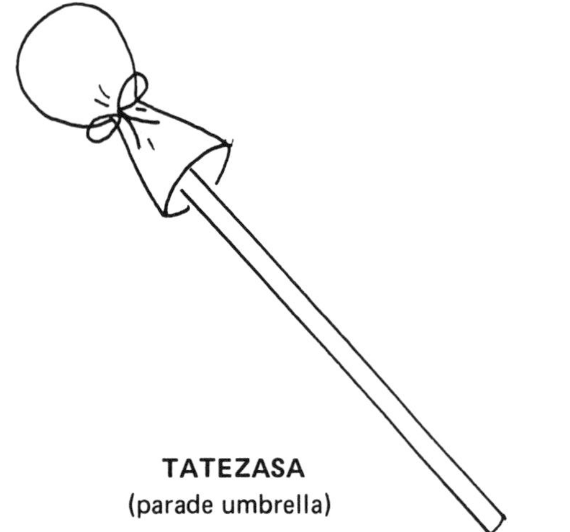

TATEZASA
(parade umbrella)

DAIZASA
(large umbrella)

SANBŌ (tray)

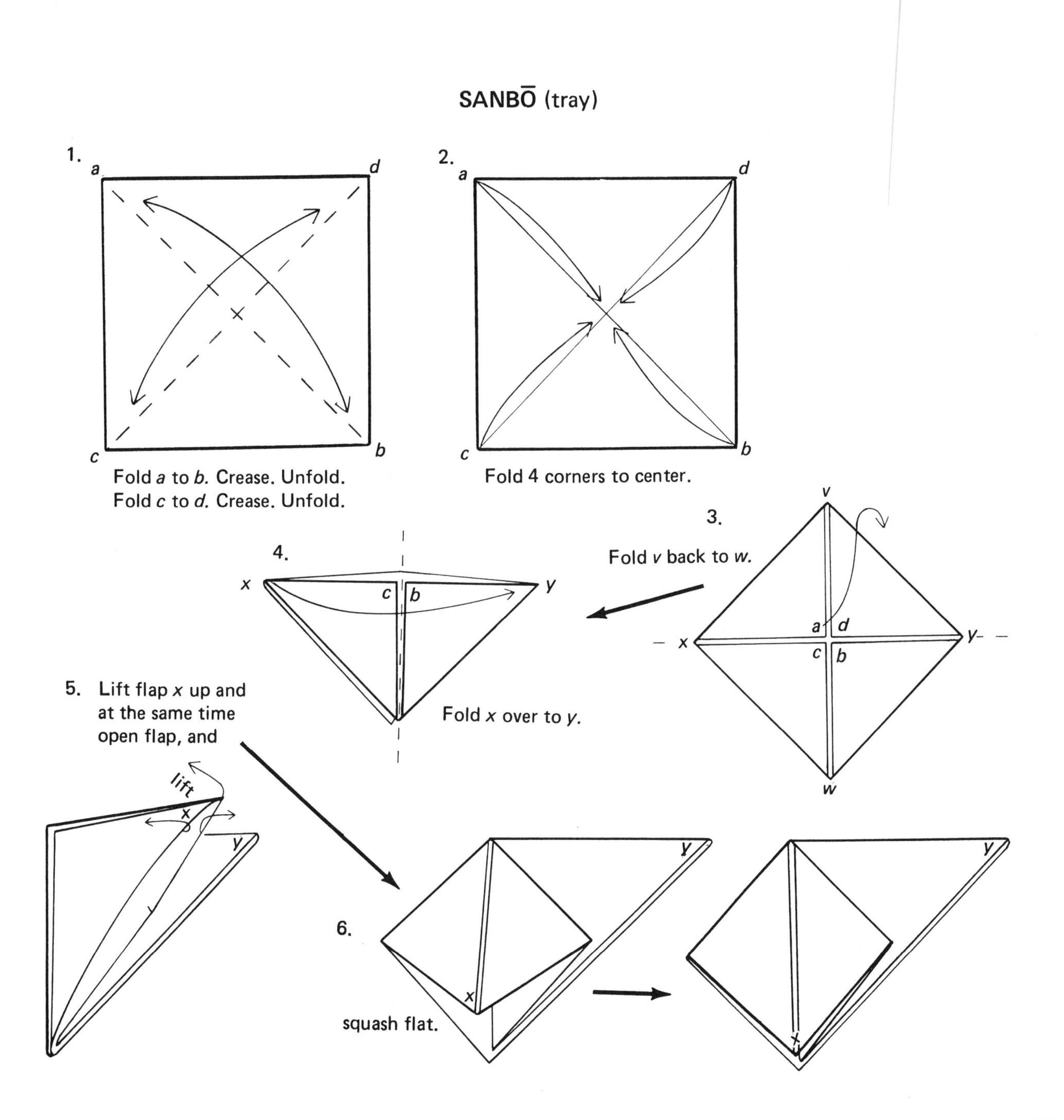
1.
a
d
c
b
Fold *a* to *b*. Crease. Unfold.
Fold *c* to *d*. Crease. Unfold.
2.
a
d
c
b
Fold 4 corners to center.
3.
v
Fold *v* back to *w*.
a
d
x
c
b
y
w
4.
x
c
b
y
Fold *x* over to *y*.
5. Lift flap *x* up and
at the same time
open flap, and
lift
x
y
6.
y
x
squash flat.
y
x

7.

Turn over.
Repeat steps 5 and 6 with flap *y.*

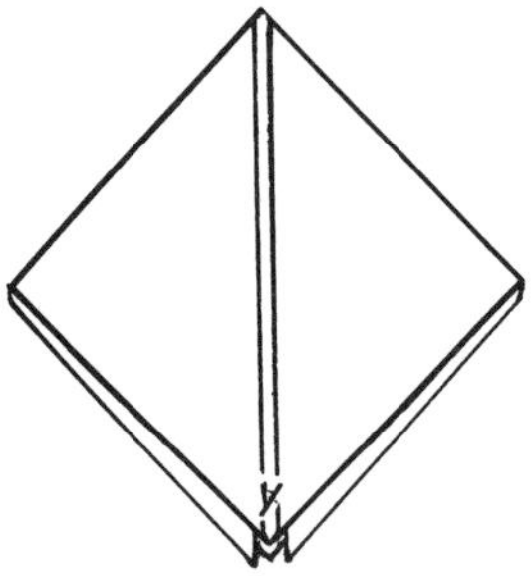

8.

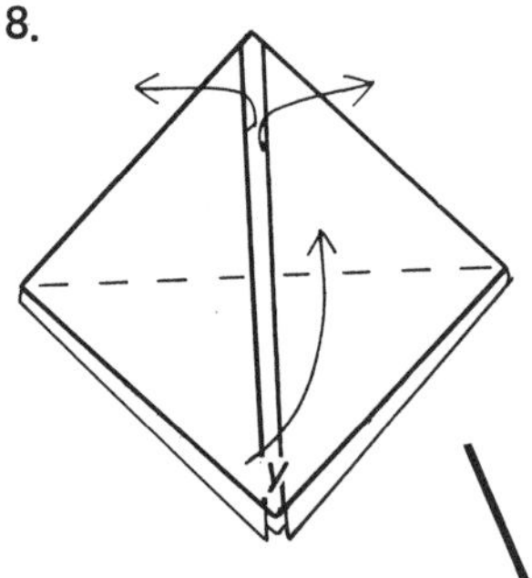

Fold flap *y* up and at the same time open flap outwards.

10.

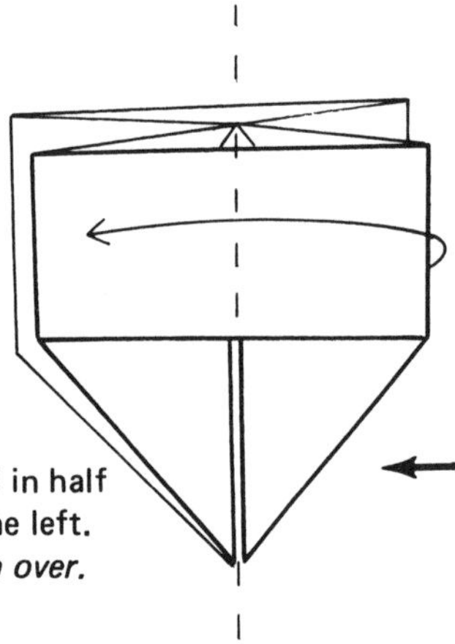

Fold in half to the left.
Turn over.

9.

Turn over.
Repeat step 8 with flap *x.*

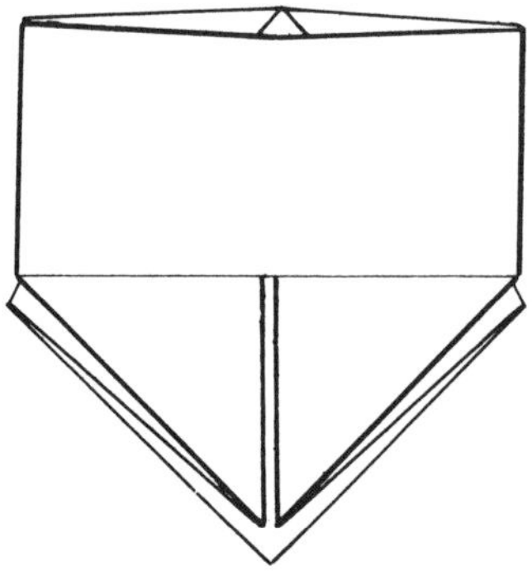

11.

Repeat step 10:
Fold in half to the left. Turn upside down.

12.

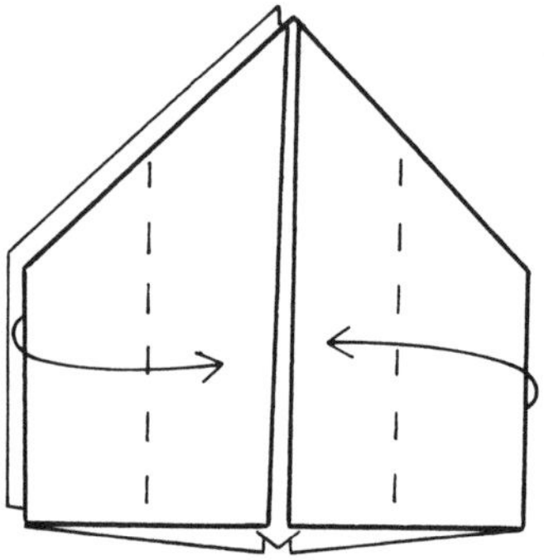

Fold sides to center.

13.

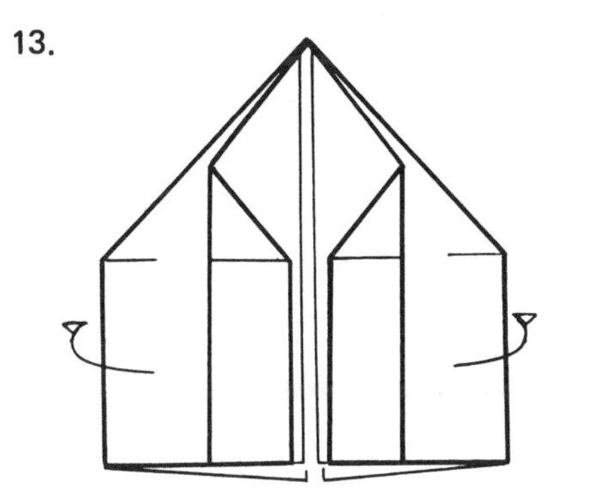

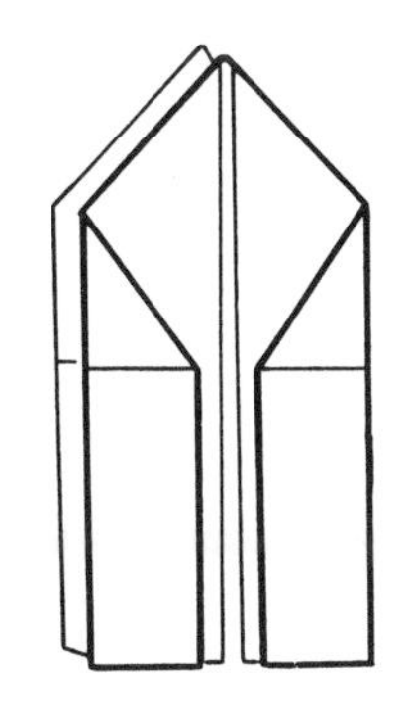

Turn over.
Fold remaining 2 sides
to center.

14.

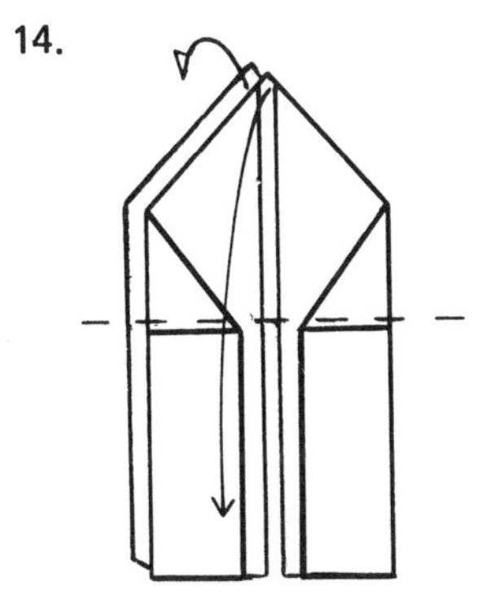

Fold top flaps out.

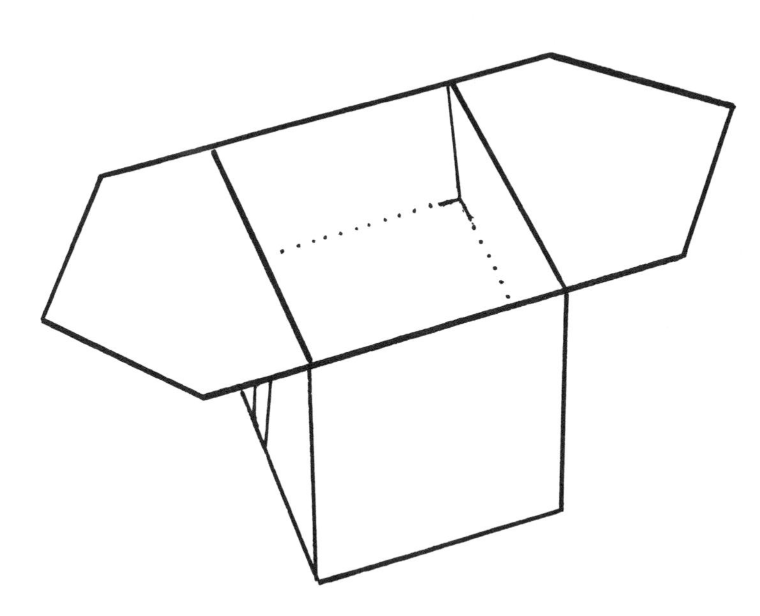

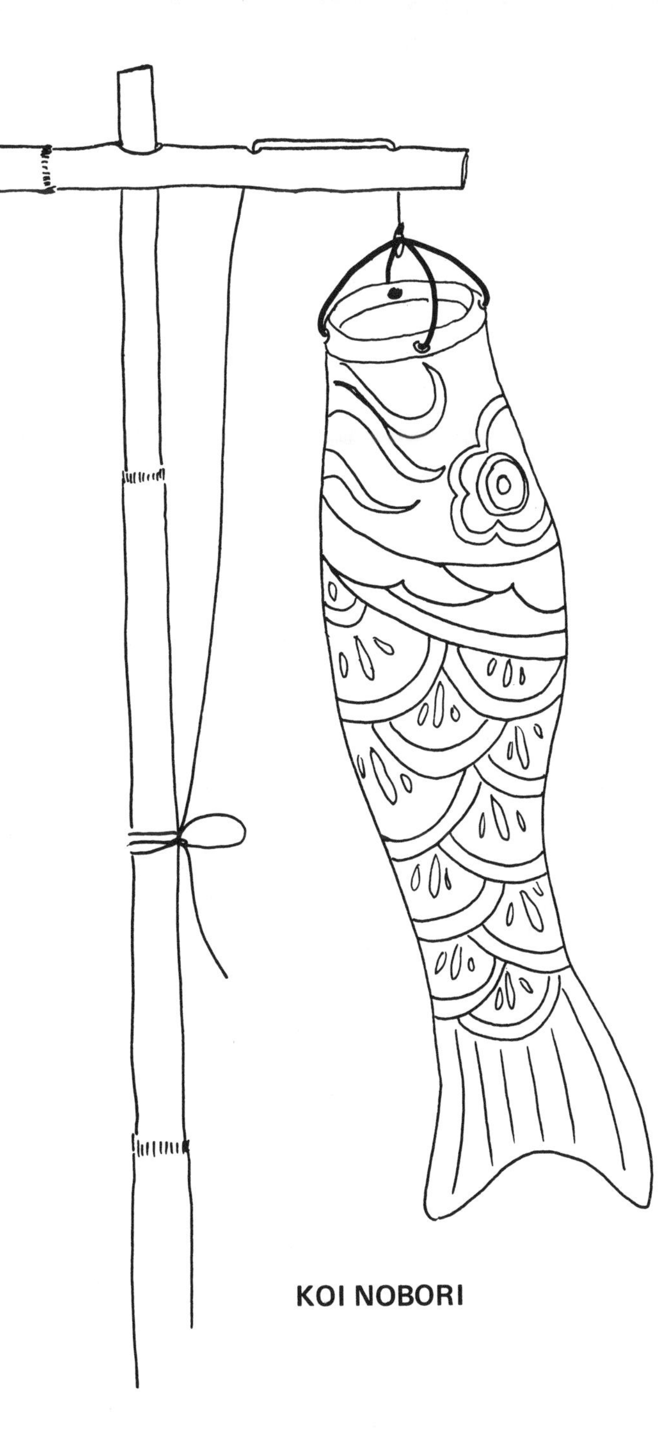

KOI NOBORI

TANGO NO SEKKU

Kodomo No Hi (Children's Day, national Japanese holiday) falls on May 5th. It shares the date with *Tango No Sekku* (Boys' day, or Boys' Festival*), which is the traditional Japanese holiday, falling on the 5th day of the 5th lunar month.

In 1948, Japan adopted a new national holiday, *Kodomo No Hi*, to promote the welfare and well-being of children, and in 1951, a Children's Constitution was adopted. On *Kodomo No Hi* special ceremonies are held bringing together children's organizations, like the Scouts, youth clubs and school representatives, to honor and give recognition to the children of Japan. In Tokyo, a children's garden party is held at the Shinjuku Gyoen (Shinjuku Park). Although this modern holiday has combined a celebration of both boys and girls, the dominant theme of May 5th still appears as *Tango No Sekku* (Boys' day or Boys' Festival).

In the United States, *Kodomo No Hi* has not been adopted and it is *Tango No Sekku* which is celebrated. Although *Tango No Sekku* is not as popular as *Hinamatsuri*, some Japanese American families display various *musha ningyō* (folk hero dolls), miniature *kabuto* (warrior's helmet), *katana* (swords), as well as fly the *koi nobori* (carp streamers) from flagpoles in their yards. Local Japanese American confectionery shops make the traditional sweets of this festival, *chimaki* (sweet, pounded rice cake, wrapped in bamboo leaf) and *kashiwamochi* (sweet bean-filled rice cake, wrapped in oak leaf). The bamboo symbolizes constancy and devotion, and the oak, strength and protectiveness. Various stores display *koi nobori* (carp streamers) and miniature "set" displays for Boys' Day.

The literal translation of *Tango No Sekku* is "Feast of (Zodiacal) Horse Day", which corresponds to the 5th day of the 5th lunar month. Originally, this day was celebrated for the health and welfare of everyone, not just boys. Herbs were gathered and made into *kusudama* (a medicinal ball), and hung in the home as a charm against disease and illness.

Some historians feel that the *Tango No Sekku* is an outgrowth of the influence of the Chinese celebration, *Sechie* (a custom where royal guards wore ceremonial military garb), which was popular in the Japanese courts dating back to 593 A.D., and the custom practiced by farmers in the 5th lunar month of frightening evil spirits and insects from harming young plants by use of bright banners and figures.

By the Tokugawa Era (1603-1868) this festival was a means to stimulate the martial spirit. Heirlooms of the *daimyō* (feudal lord of a province) and *samurai* (warrior) ancestors, such as *yoroi* (body armor), *kabuto* (helmet), *katana* (sword) and *sashimono*

*Sometimes called *Shōbu No Sekku* (Iris Festival).

(banner-standards), were brought out and displayed outside of the home. Historical deeds and battles engaged by the family ancestors, as well as famous battles in history, were told to the sons so that they would know and carry on the family honor and traditions. Class distinction was rigid, and farmers and merchants could not observe this festival in an elaborate way, but during the peaceful Genroku Era (1700's), new ideas and attitudes developed and *Tango No Sekku* emerged as a festival for all boys. It was not until the early 19th Century that the displays were brought into the household and displayed on the *tokonoma* (alcove). *Musha ningyō* (dolls representing famous feudal lords, *samurai*, folk heroes, both fictional and real) developed and became part of the display.

Shōbu No Sekku (Iris Festival) is another name for this festival. The flower symbolizes "uprightness" by the unbending way it sits on the stem, while the leaves are considered to be spiritual weapons by which evil can be overcome. Wooden toy swords displayed on this day are called *shōbu katana* (iris swords). The word *shōbu* also has a meaning of being successful, to be a winner. *Shōbu-yu* or *ayame no yu* (bath made from water boiled with iris leaves and roots) are taken by the boys to instill the *samurai* spirit and to prevent illness during the summer months. This practice of taking *shōbu-yu* originated in the Muromachi Era (1392-1490), gaining much popularity in the Edo Era (1603-1868). Even today, *sento* (public baths) have *shōbu-yu* on May 5th.

The flying of the *koi nobori* (carp streamers) and *fukinagashi* (colored streamers) started during the Anei Era (1722-1780). This custom of hoisting huge streamers from tall poles in the yards of households with sons gained rapid popularity and is still a popular display in Japan. The *koi* (carp) is a symbol of aspiration, daring and success. The word *koi* also means, when written in different *kanji* (ideographs), "purpose" and "love", as in dutiful love towards parents. The *koi nobori* is usually made of cloth or heavy paper and colored red, symbolizing vitality and the color of the sun; or black, for fertility and the color of rain clouds. The largest *koi nobori*, usually red in color and as long as 15 feet or more, is traditionally for the eldest son, with the other *koi* grading down in size.

Fukinagashi (red and white, or multicolored streamers) probably came directly from the early use of chasing away evil spirits from crops. The term literally means "flowing-blown". *Fuki* also means free, unrestrained life.

The *sashimono* (banner-standard) was originally used as instruments of exorcism in ancient Japan. The temples later used special *sashimono* in a ceremony called *tateage* (lifting up), where a boy of seven celebrated his transition from childhood to boyhood. *Sashimono* of a warrior had his family crest or the crest of his *tono-sama* (feudal lord) printed on it. These all later evolved to the *sashimono* decorated with figures of heroes and animals.

Unlike the *Hinamatsuri* display, there is no prescribed form of regulating the Boys' Day display. The exhibit need only be a few

MOMOTARO

bugu (old style military implements) which are placed on the *tokonoma* or on a 3 to 5 tiered stand, which is covered with a green cloth. The green cloth is used as a symbol of fertility and the color of vegetation (freshness) and of water, which is believed to be the source of life.

Display models that can be incorporated are: (on the top step) *andon* (ancient oil lamps), which stand for vigilance; *yoroi* (body armor), with helmet and leggings, sitting on the *yoroi bitsu* (the storage container for the armor); *yari* (spear, lance), *yumi* (bow) and *ya* (arrows), *daitō* (long sword) and *wakizashi* (short sword)*; *sashimono* (martial banners and flags); camp curtains, as used by warriors of old for enclosures. On the second step: *shōbu* (iris); *sanbō* (tray stand) with *kashiwa-mochi* and *chimaki dango* (traditional sweets of the festival); *kabuto* (helmet), or *jingasa* (war hat); *gunsen* (leader's fan); *saihai* (short stick, a commander's baton); *sake* (rice wine). On the third step: *Shōki* (protector of the people from evil influence and devil expeller); a white horse, the emblem of the day, symbolizing manliness, courage, strength, fertility, as well as being a protective spirit; a tiger, symbolizing all that is powerful and the forces of nature both creative and destructive. On the fourth and fifth steps are placed the various *musha ningyō*.

Some of the more famous *musha ningyō* are: Yoshitsune, young, valiant general of the Minamoto Clan during the Gempei Wars (12th Century); Benkei, gigantic servant and follower of Yoshitsune, whose power and strength and loyalty are much admired; Kusunoki Masahige, known also as Dai Nanko, a great and faithful warrior who died in the cause of his emperor after the Battle of Minatogawa in 1336; Minamoto Yorimitsu, famous warrior of the year 1000, who saved the Kyoto area from being plundered by evil; Hachiman Taro Yoshīe, who distinguished himself with military deeds in the mid-11th Century; Toyotomi Hideyoshi, the peasant boy who rose to become the *Shōgun* (generalissimo) at the end of the 16th Century; Tokugawa Ieyasu, founder of the shogunal line of 250 years; Jinmu Tenno, traditional founder of the Japanese empire in 660 B.C.; Kintarō or Kintoki, the infant-Hercules of Japanese folklore; Momotarō, storybook boy-hero whose feats made him *Nippon Ichi* (First in Japan) among all the heroes.

**Katana* is the generic term for 'sword'.

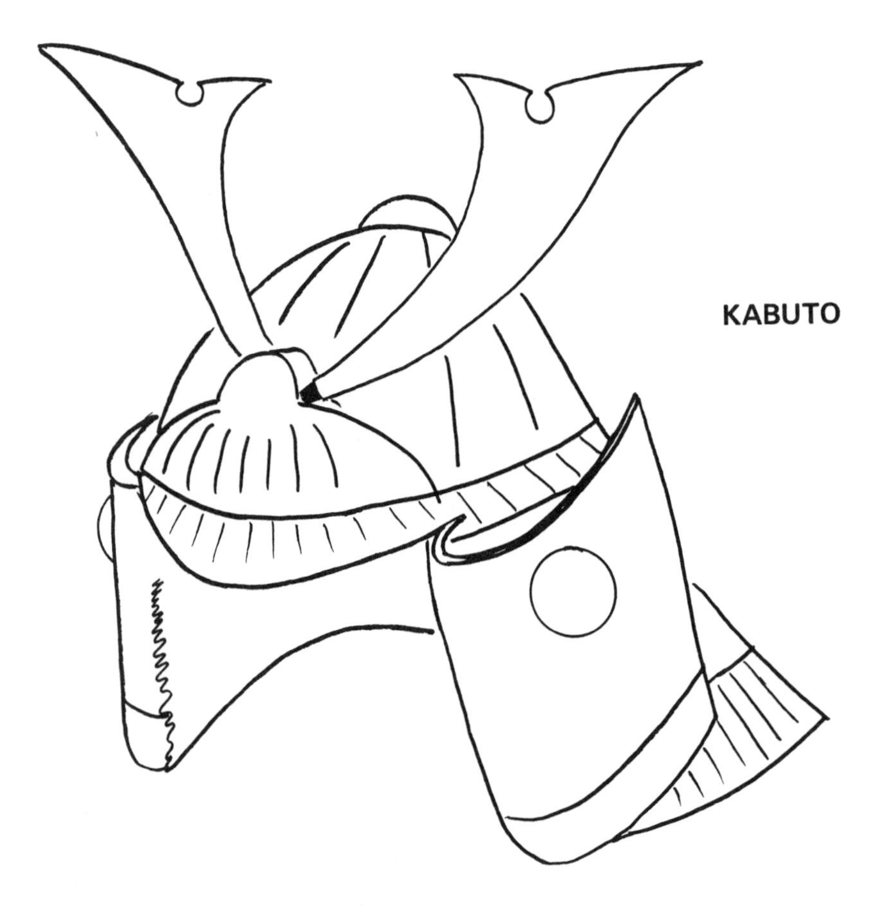
KABUTO

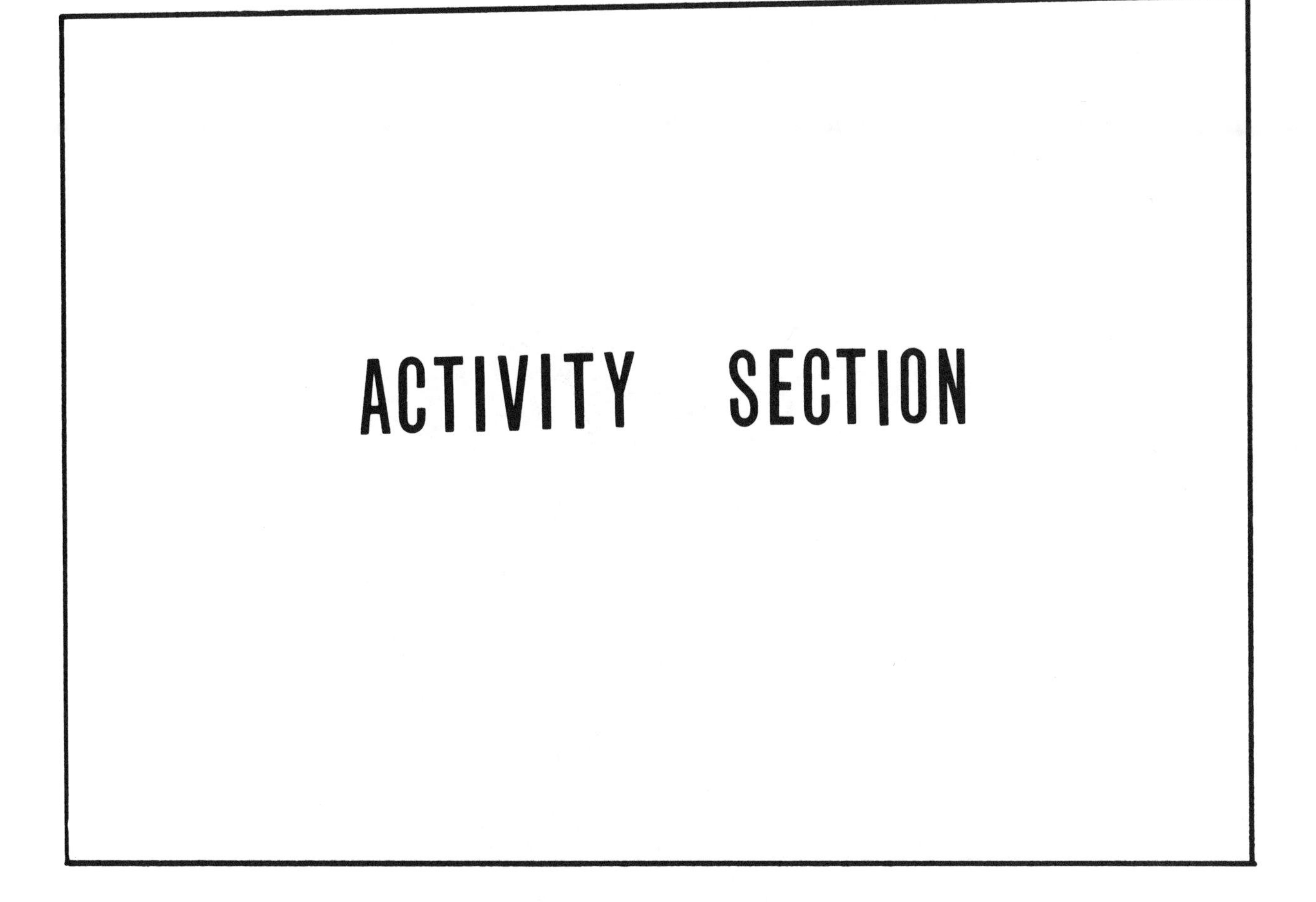

ACTIVITY SECTION

TANGO NO SEKKU

The display developed here for *Tango No Sekku* (Boys' Day) is relatively easy and inexpensive, uses readily available materials, and employs a diversity of approaches, including sewing, baking, paper-folding, painting, sculpturing, and woodworking.

Displays differ in content and number of objects. The one given here consists of:

- two *fukinagashi* (streamers, in two different styles)
- *sashimono* (banner)
- *koi nobori* (carp streamer)
- *yoroi* (body armor) and accessories
- *kabuto* (helmet)
- *shōbu* (iris flower)

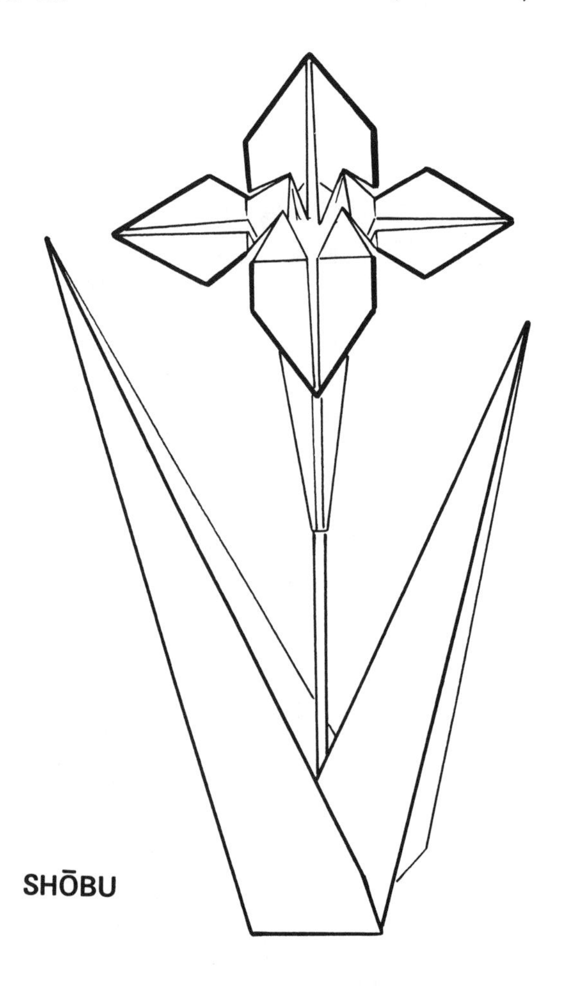

SHŌBU

TANGO NO SEKKU

The overall project is like this:

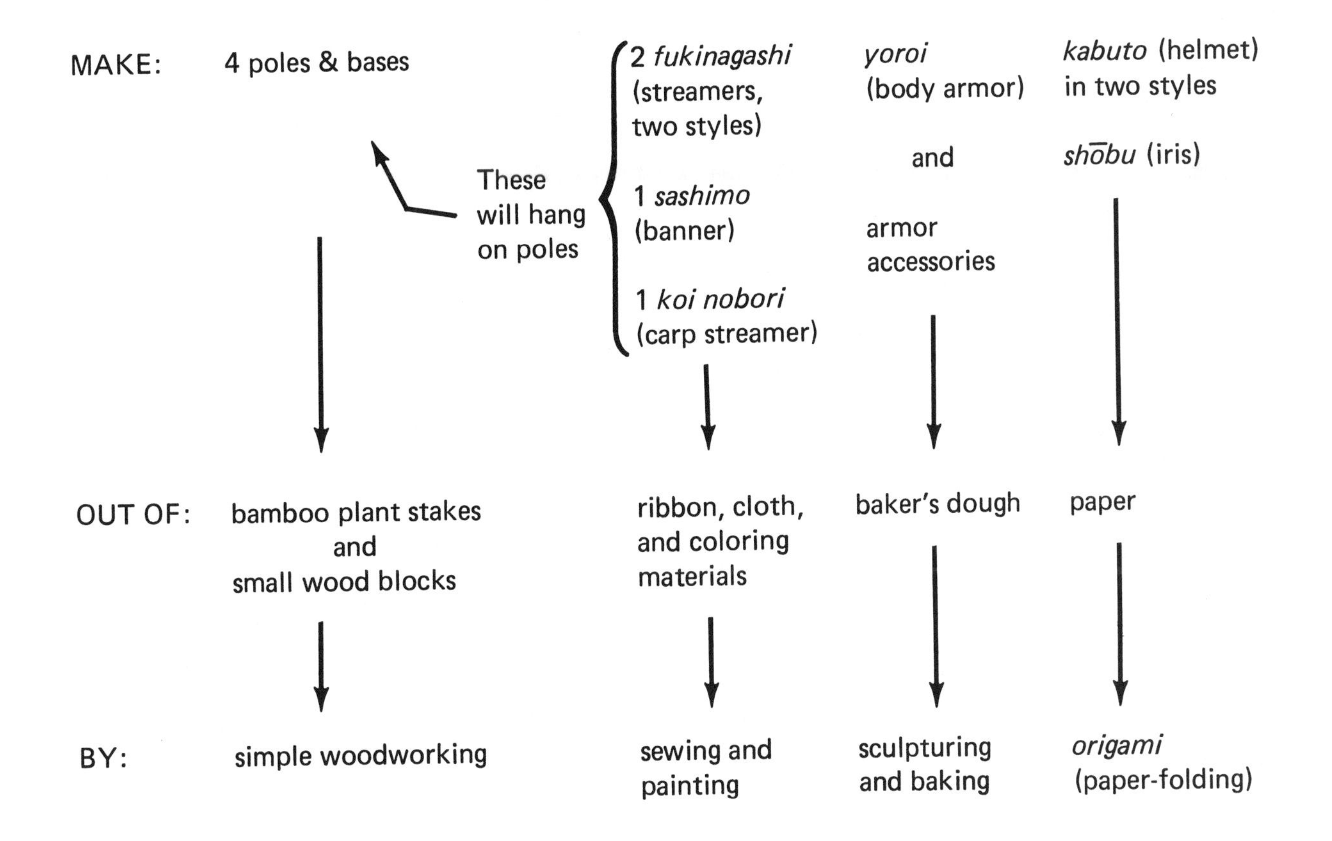

POLES

for

2 *fukinagashi* (streamers)
1 *sashimono* (banner)
1 *koi nobori* (carp streamer)

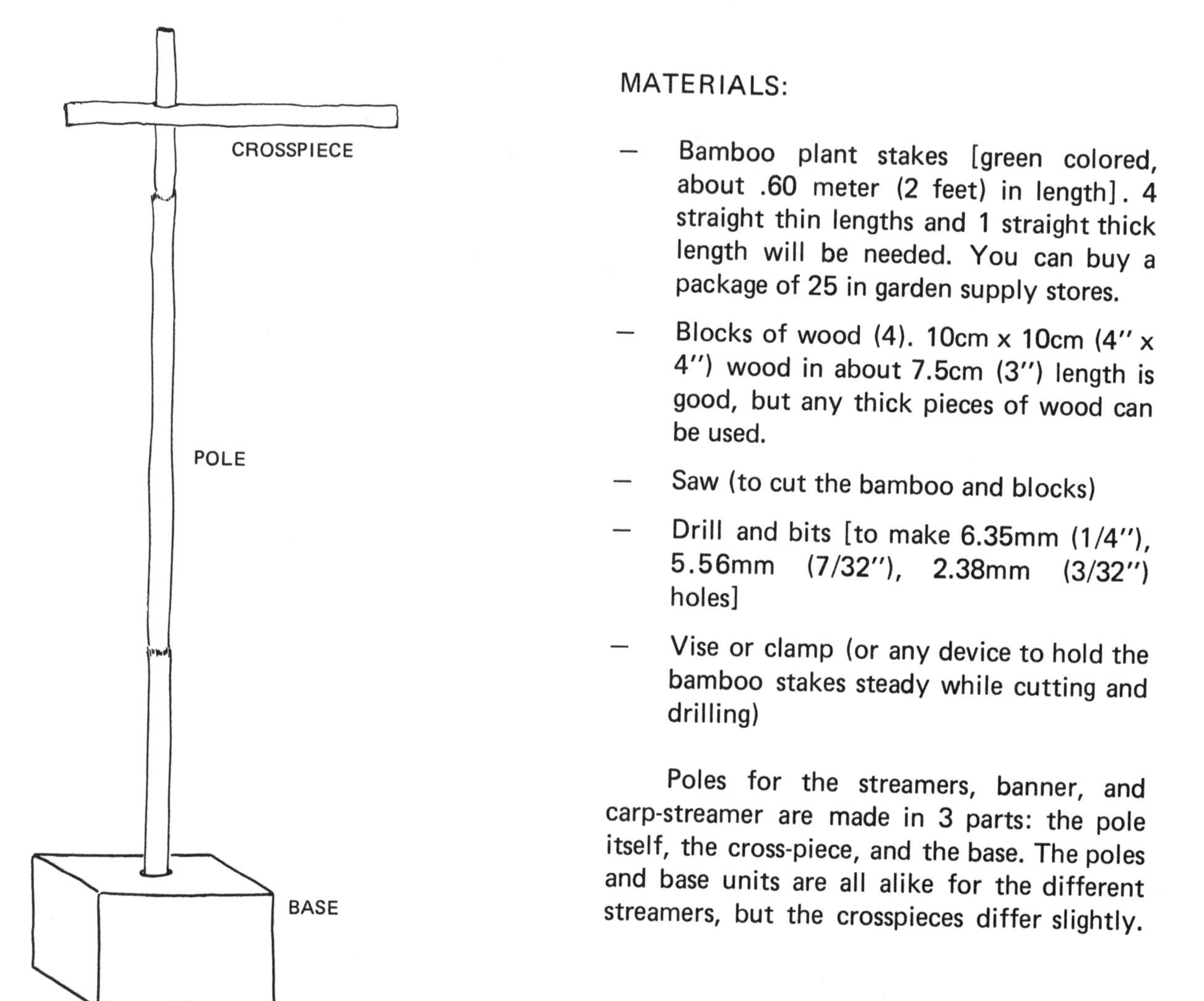

MATERIALS:

— Bamboo plant stakes [green colored, about .60 meter (2 feet) in length]. 4 straight thin lengths and 1 straight thick length will be needed. You can buy a package of 25 in garden supply stores.

— Blocks of wood (4). 10cm x 10cm (4" x 4") wood in about 7.5cm (3") length is good, but any thick pieces of wood can be used.

— Saw (to cut the bamboo and blocks)

— Drill and bits [to make 6.35mm (1/4"), 5.56mm (7/32"), 2.38mm (3/32") holes]

— Vise or clamp (or any device to hold the bamboo stakes steady while cutting and drilling)

Poles for the streamers, banner, and carp-streamer are made in 3 parts: the pole itself, the cross-piece, and the base. The poles and base units are all alike for the different streamers, but the crosspieces differ slightly.

POLES:

– 4 lengths of bamboo [they should already be about .60 meter (2 feet) long]. Select thin and straight lengths.

BASE:

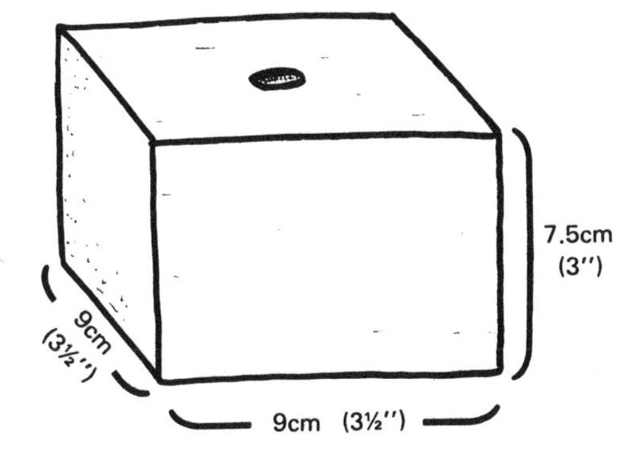

Cut out of four-by-four wood [which is actually 9cm x 9cm (3-1/2" x 3-1/2"), 4 lengths of about 7.5cm (3")].

Drill a 6.35mm (1/4") hole in the center about 3.7cm (1-1/2") in depth into each base unit.

Sand and stain, if desired.

(Any size block of wood can be used, but if it is too small, the pole may tip over or just appear too small.)

CROSSPIECES: In the diagram on the ing page, make two "A", one "B", "C" crosspieces.

3 different types of crosspieces are made from a thick bamboo stake. It must be thick enough for a hole, about 5.56mm (7/32") in width, in which the pole will fit.

In sawing the bamboo to lengths, keep turning the bamboo (as you saw) so that the final sawing occurs in the middle of the cut. This will avoid splintering.

To make the hole for the pole, clamp the crosspiece in a vise firmly, and drill a small hole [e.g. with a 2.38mm (3/32") bit] in the correct position. Then drill a 5.56mm (7/32") hole using the small hole as a guide. [The size of the hole need not be exactly 5.56mm (7/32"). Any size slightly larger than the top of the pole is okay.] Also, the size of the small holes for crosspiece "A" need not be precisely 2.38mm (3/32") ... just large enough to pass thread through.

ASSEMBLY:

– Put the pole into the hole in the base unit.

– Put the crosspiece on the pole. The crosspiece should not slip down below about 5cm (2") from the top of the pole. Usually a node or a slight curvature

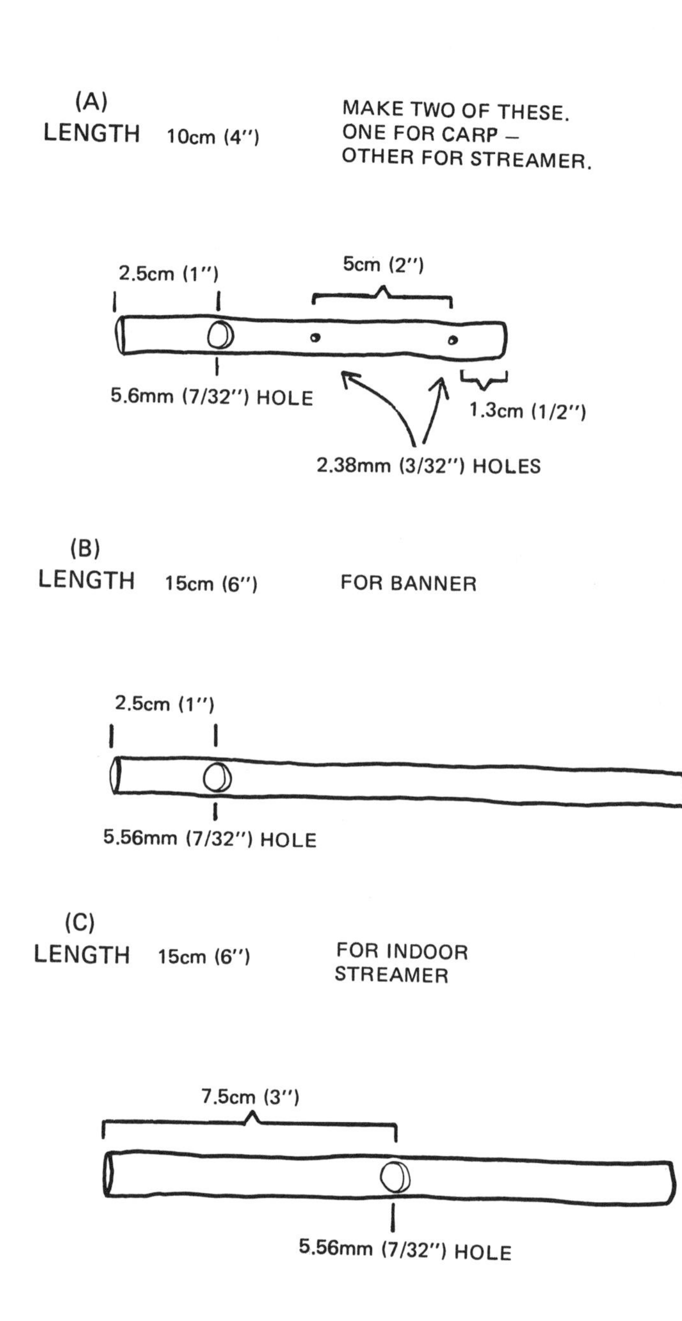

in the pole will prevent the crosspiece from slipping too low. Different pole or different size hole may have to be used. A small amount of experimenting will lead to a snug fitting crosspiece. (Toothpick to jam the hole or glue can be used, but do not do so for the banner crosspiece ("B") until after the banner is placed on the pole.

FUKINAGASHI
(streamers) for INDOOR DISPLAY

MATERIALS:

- Ribbon, 2cm (3/4") width, the type used for gift wrapping. 5 different colors: green, white, red, yellow, and dark blue or purple or black. [About 1 meter (36") of each color will be used.]
- Gold document seals or ornaments (2) (type used for Christmas gift wrapping is fine).
- Scissors
- Stapler
- White glue

ASSEMBLY:

Cut ribbons to about 1 meter (36") long, fold in half and staple the ribbon so that a loop is formed. The ribbon is placed on the crosspiece of the pole through the loop. For the middle ribbon, a hole must be cut to fit over the pole. The order of color is unimportant. Staple ribbon from outside at bottom of crossbar; fasten the middle ribbon with tape on both sides (see illustration pp. 92). After placing the ribbons on the crosspiece, glue on gold ornaments near the ends of the crosspiece.

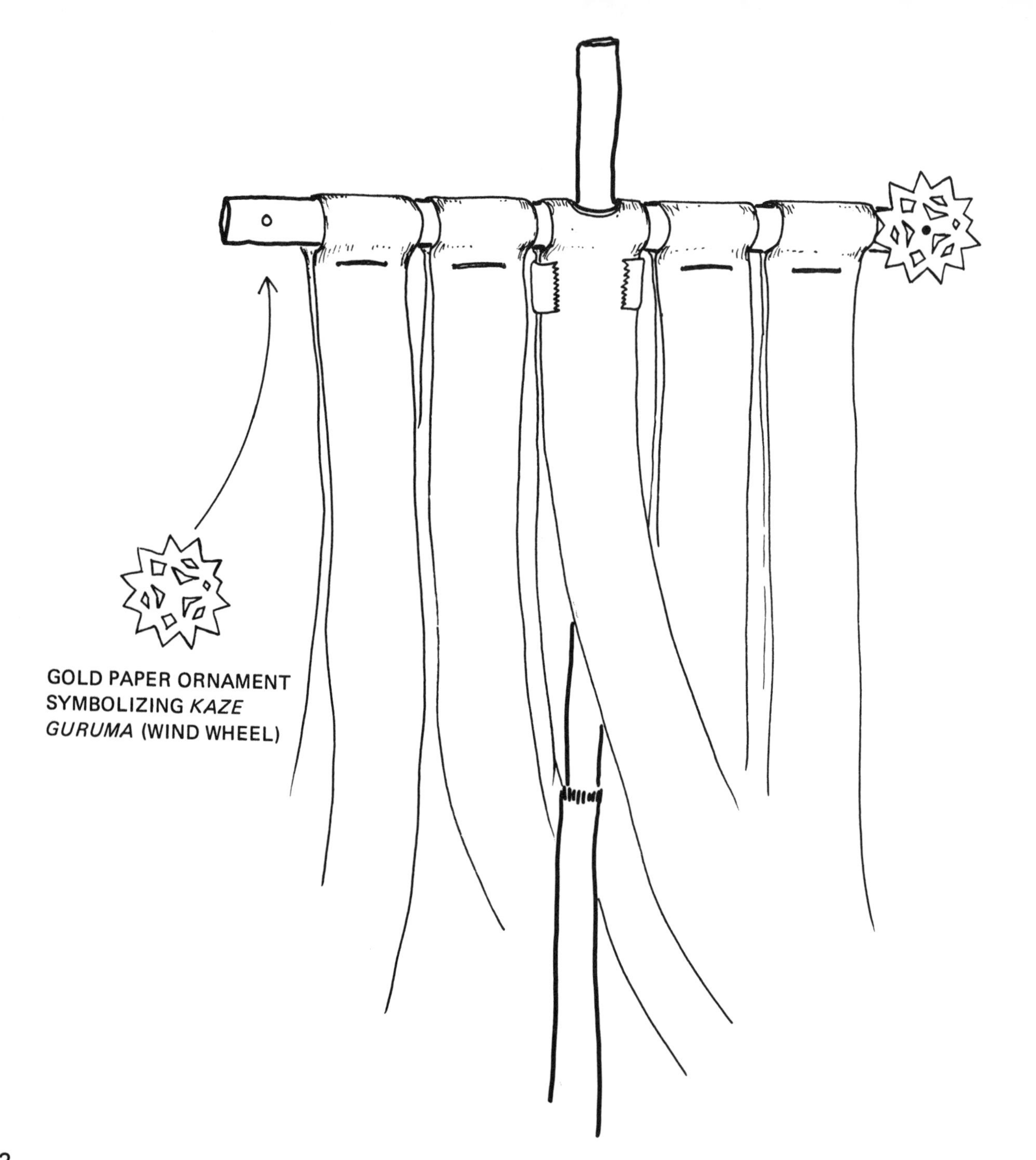
GOLD PAPER ORNAMENT
SYMBOLIZING *KAZE*
GURUMA (WIND WHEEL)

FUKINAGASHI
(streamer) for DISPLAYING ON POLE

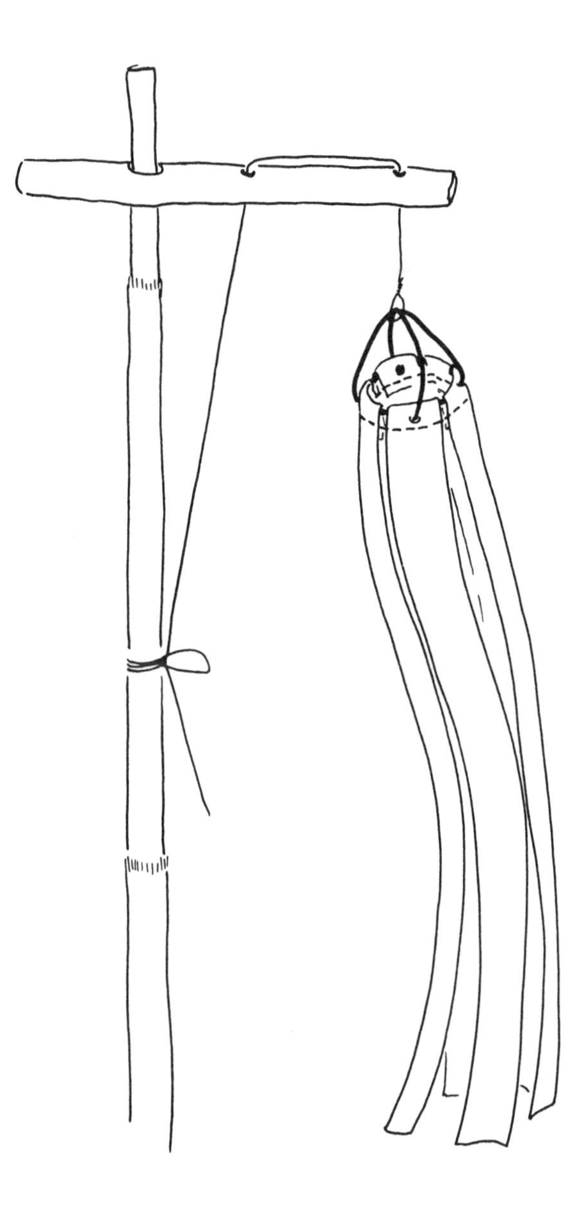

MATERIALS:

- Ribbon, 2cm (3/4") width (the type used for gift wrapping). 5 different colors: green, white, red, yellow, and dark blue or purple or black. [About .50 meter (18") of each color will be used.]
- Thin wire, about 12.5cm (5") in length
- Heavy thread for harness and flagpole line
- Needle and thread
- Wire cutter
- Pointed-nose pliers

ASSEMBLY:

Fold tops of ribbons to a 1.3cm (1/2") hem. Stitch by hand, connecting the ribbons together. (Back stitching is stronger.)

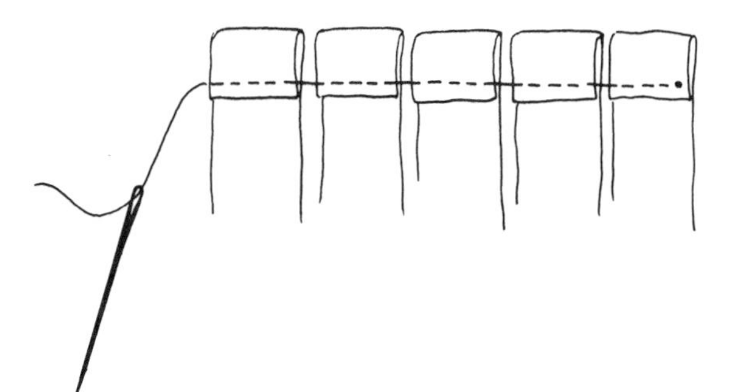

Thread wire through the loops formed by hemming the ribbons, and twist closed, forming a circle. Stitch to connect the two end ribbons together to secure the circle (see illustration).

Make harness, using needle and heavy thread. Tie flagpole line to harness and HOIST . . .

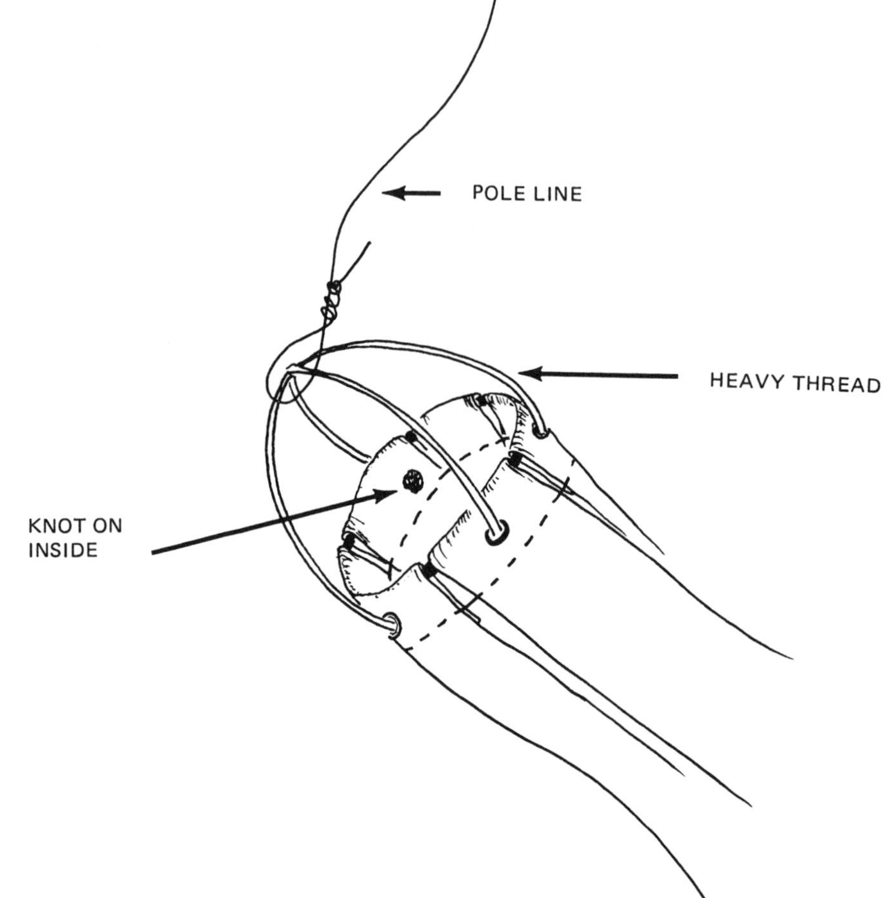

SASHIMONO (banner)

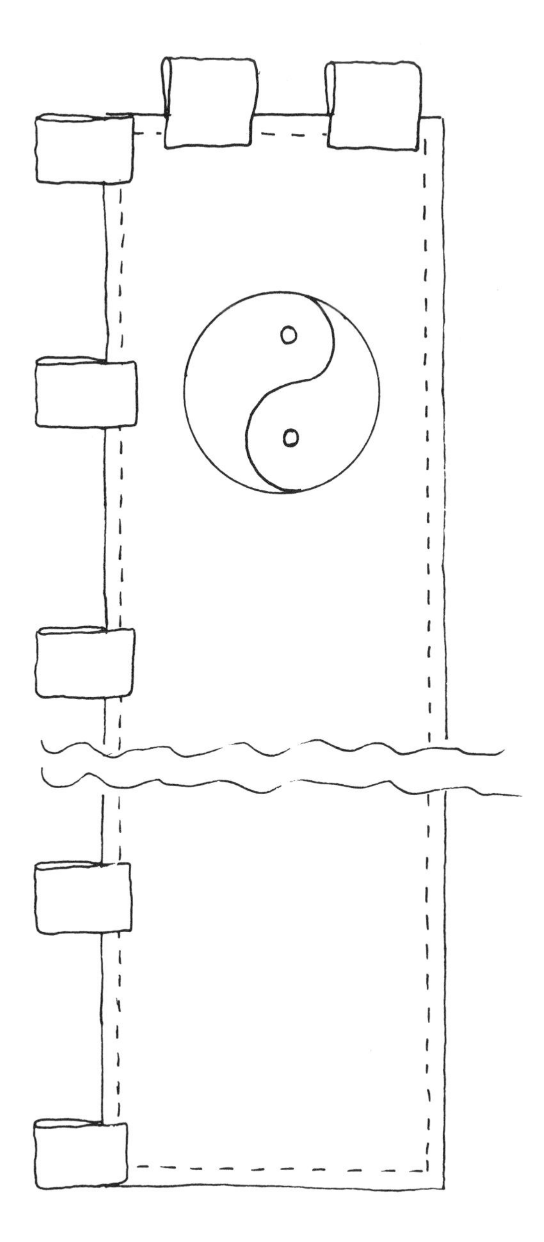

MATERIALS:

- White cloth (old sheets will do)
- White thread, needle, pins
- Permanent marking felt pens, any color will do
- Tape measure, ruler
- Sewing machine, if available

ASSEMBLY:

BANNER: Cut cloth into 43.5cm x 12.5cm (17" x 5"). Turn 6.35mm (1/4") raw edge in, all around, and turn another 6.35mm (1/4") for finished edge. Stitch by hand or machine.

Draw a design on the banner in pencil and color in with felt marking pens. The ink will run into the cloth. The amount of running will depend on the cloth and how quickly the strokes are made. Take this running into account when coloring the design, perhaps by experimenting on scraps of the cloth.

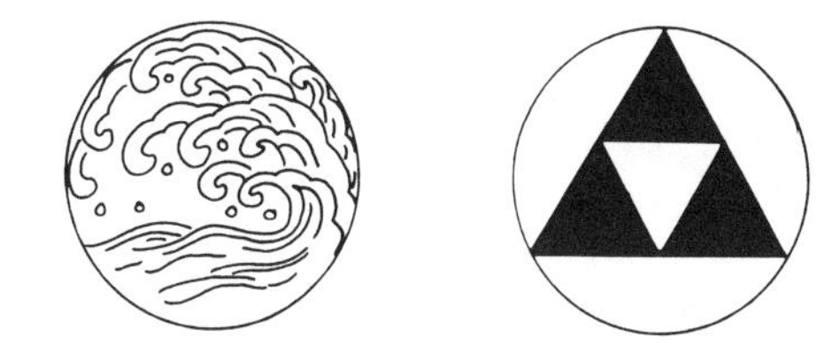

BANNER LOOPS:

FOR SIDE LOOPS (5 of them), cut a 3.7cm x 38.0cm (1-1/2" x 15") piece of cloth, fold in half and stitch a 6.35mm (1/4") seam. Turn inside out, and cut into five 7cm (2-3/4") strips. Fold strips in half and place, evenly spaced, on left side of banner. Attach, leaving 1.3cm (1/2") loop free for threading on pole. Tuck 1cm (3/8") of raw edge inward for a finished edge. Stitch by hand or machine.

FOR TOP LOOPS (2 of them), cut 5cm x 14cm (2" x 5-1/2") piece of cloth. Sew as same for side loops, but leaving 2.3cm (7/8") loop free for crosspiece threading.

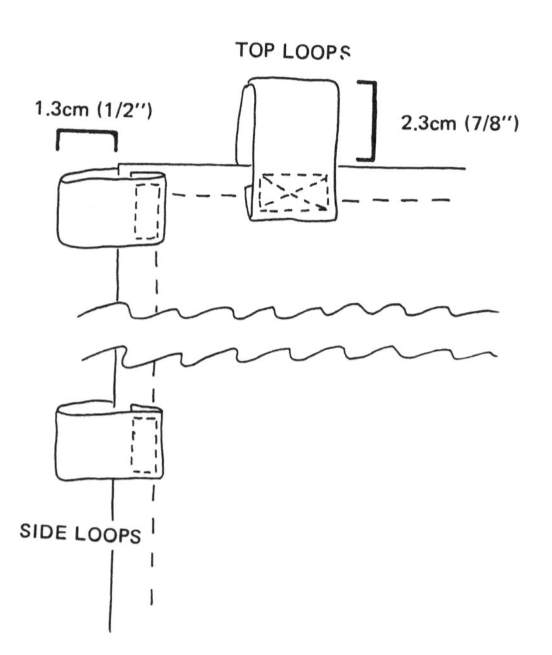

Now, HOIST THE *SASHIMONO* UP THE POLE . . .

KOI NOBORI
(carp streamer)

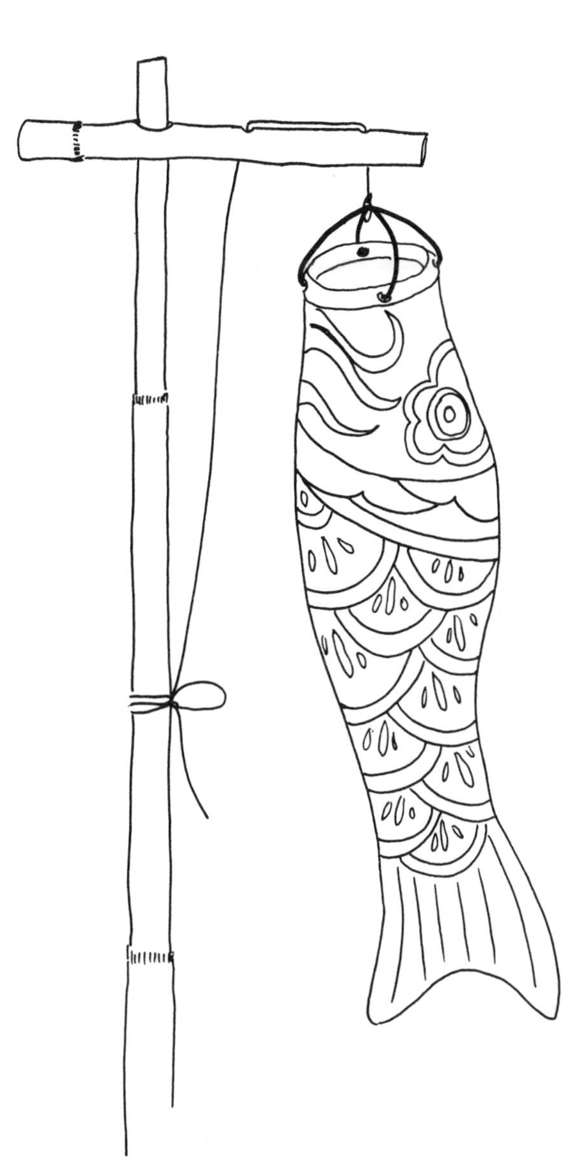

MATERIALS:

- White cloth (old sheets will do)
- Heavy thread for harness and pole line
- Permanent marking felt pens, your choice of colors
- Needle and white thread
- Scissors
- Thin wire and wire cutter
- Pointed nose pliers
- Pencil
- Sewing machine, if available

ASSEMBLY:

CARP: Fold cloth in half, cut to desired length. (Fish pattern on page 99 may be used.) Sketch design on cloth with pencil, and color in with marking felt pens. (Refer to notes on color running of ink on page 95.)

Fold the cloth so that the coloring is on the inside. Stitch (by hand or machine) along the open edge. Do NOT stitch the mouth or tail openings. Turn the fish right side out.

Form a circle with wire, the same diameter as mouth. Turn a finished hem around the wire. Sew hem by hand.

Make harness as shown in illustration on page 94. Tie pole line to harness and HOIST UP THE *KOI NOBORI* . . .

When making a very large *koi nobori*, liquid dye can be used for coloring, but be careful when applying because the dye spreads easily when brushed on fabric.

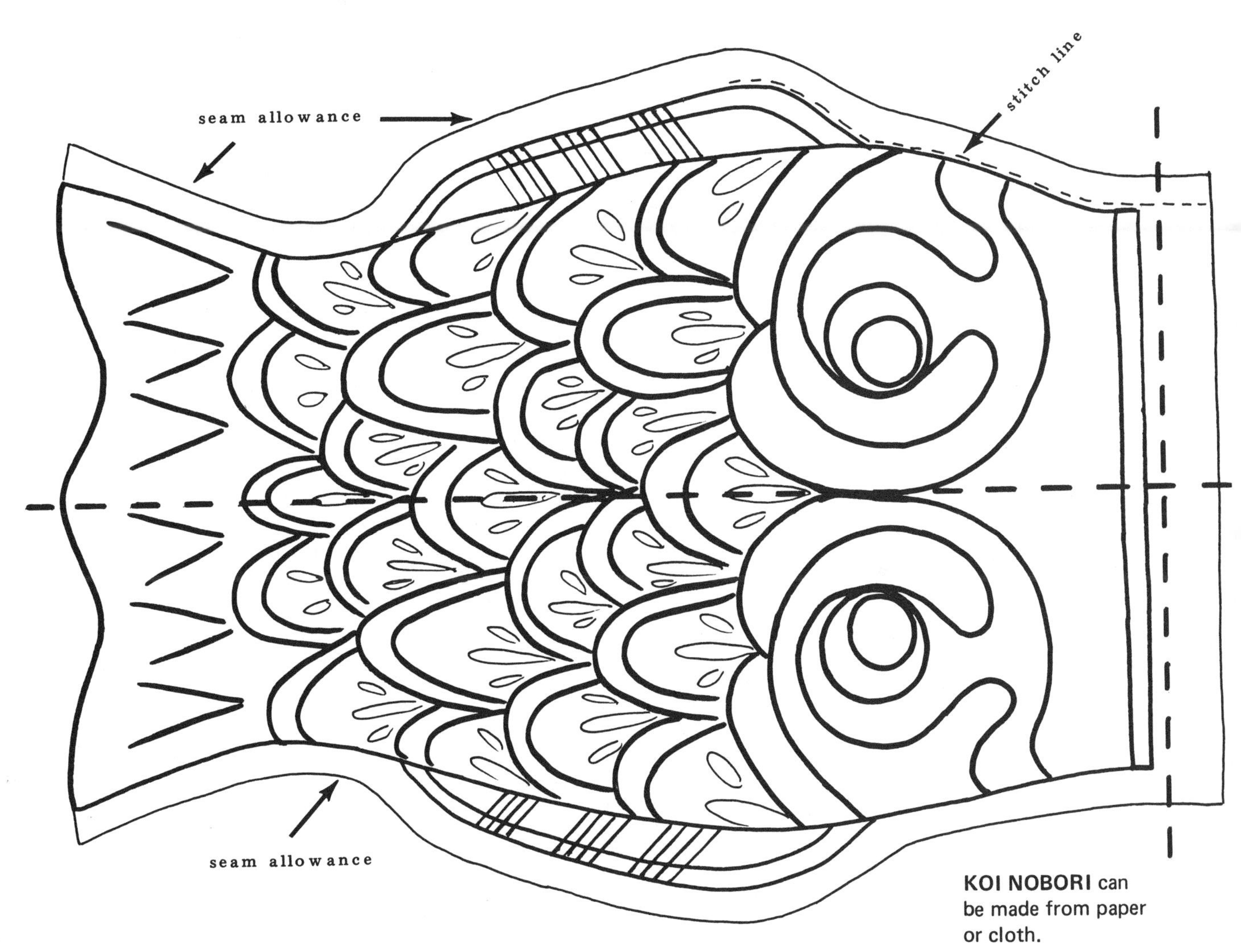

KOI NOBORI can be made from paper or cloth.

Color design with permanent marking felt pens.

USING BAKER'S DOUGH TO MAKE REPLICA OF A SUIT OF ARMOR

MATERIALS:

- flour
- salt
- water
- bowls
- rolling pin
- Scotch or masking tape
- newspaper
- pastry cloth or wax paper
- wood block (size of block depends on largeness of finished product; we used 5cm x 5cm (2" x 2") scrap lumber
- tools to etch with:

  orange stick (used in manicuring)
  clay modeling tools
  butter knife
  toothpicks

Step I: Making the Basic Form

Newspaper Form: Although a "person" is not being made, a form is needed as a base and support for the baker's dough.

Procedure:

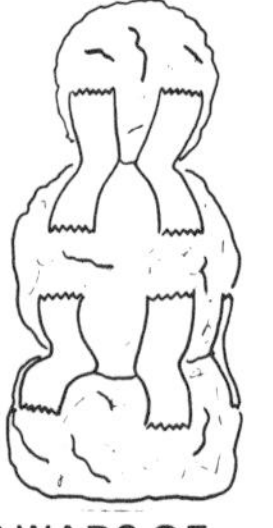

3 WADS OF NEWSPAPER

OR

2 SHEETS OF ROLLED NEWSPAPER

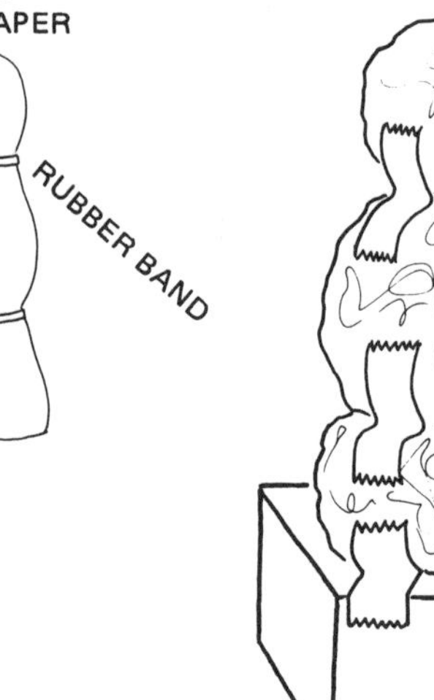

Crumple and mold sheet(s) of newspaper into a form around which the baker's dough will be applied and shaped. The torso section should be larger than the head and lower sections. Tape the pieces together and place on the wood block; secure with tape on-to the block. The wood block becomes the chest on which the armor is displayed.

Baker's Dough Recipe: (two recipes are given, either may be used)

A		B
1 liter (4 cups) flour 250ml (1 cup) salt 375ml (1-1/2 cups) water	OR	1 liter (4 cups) flour 500ml (2 cups) Masa Harina (corn flour) 375ml (1-1/2 cups) salt 500ml (2 cups) water

Mix ingredients. Knead.

Procedure: Take some of the dough and mold it evenly around the newspaper form, shaping and refining as you go. Use more of the dough to shape arms and legs (shoulder and thigh pads will be attached to these parts).

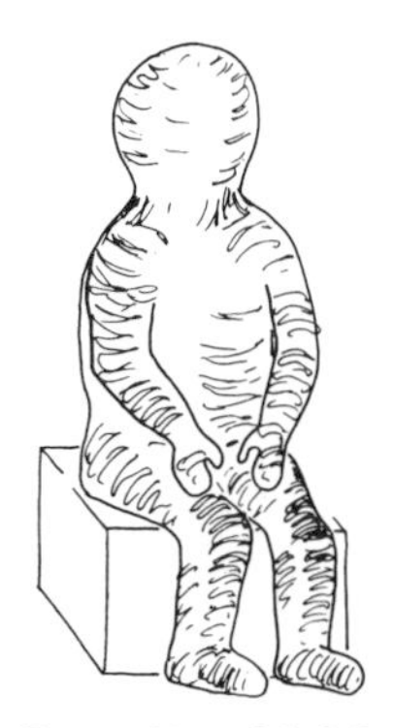

Step II: Making the Body Sheath and Panels

NOTE: Specific sizes and measurements will not be given in the following procedural steps since they will be dependent upon and proportionate to the size of the basic form you have made.

Procedure:

1) Determine the size of the body sheath and panels, proportionate to the size of the form you made.

2) Roll some of the dough flat [about 6.35mm (1/4") thick] on the pastry cloth or wax paper and outline, with the toothpick or butter knife, the following pieces:

   - 1 body sheath with straps
   - 4 skirt panels
   - 2 shoulder pads
   - 2 thigh pads

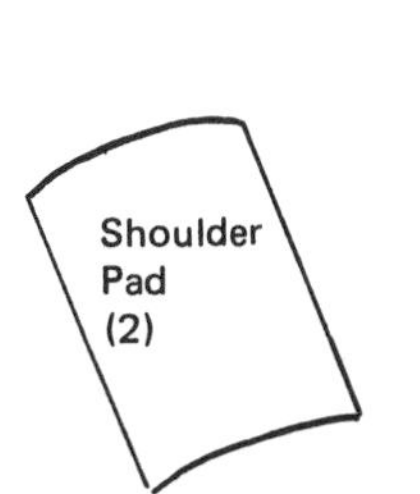

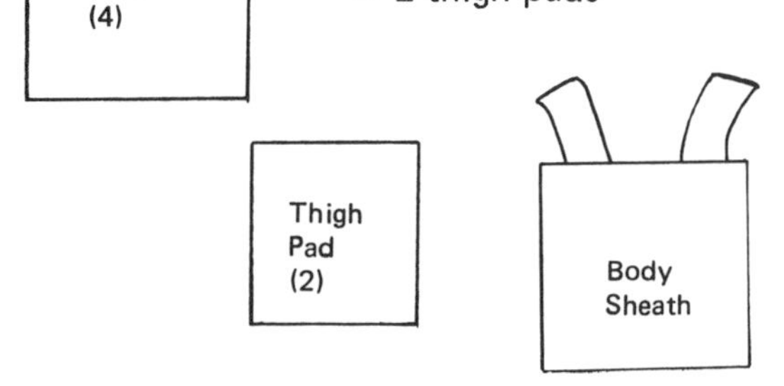

3) Cut out the pieces with a knife.

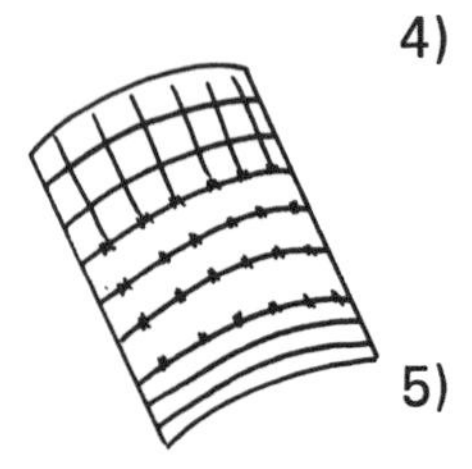

4) Etch the above pieces with a toothpick to simulate ribbings on the armor.

5) Press the sheath and panels firmly to the body form (refer to picture to get an idea of placement).

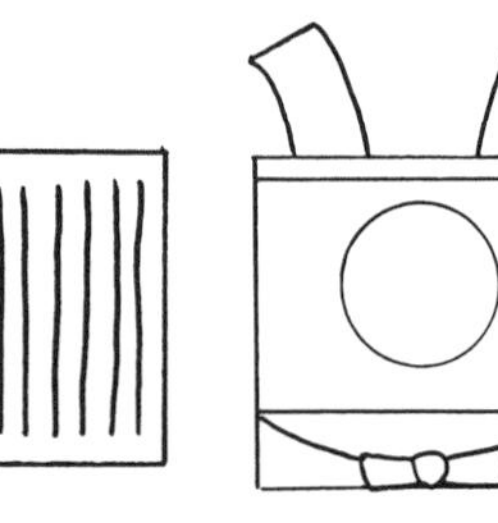

Step III: Making the Mask

Procedure:

1) Determine the size of the mask.

2) Outline the mask shape on the rolled dough and cut out.

3) Make eyes and mouth slits on the mask.

4) Attach the mask to the face section of the form. Do not press too flat, otherwise it will look like a "face" rather than a mask.

Step IV: Making the Helmet

Procedure:

1) Wad a sheet of newspaper.

2) Mold the baker's dough on top of the newspaper and shape into a helmet. Refer to the picture to get an idea of the shape and design of the helmet. The helmet should be proportionate to the basic form.

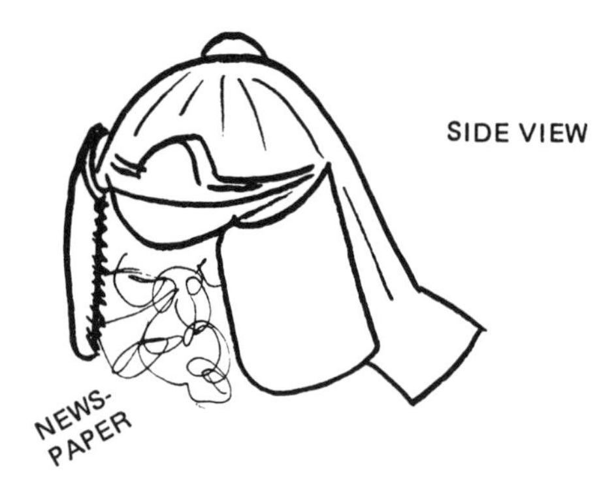

3) Shape 2 sickles out of the dough.

4) Insert a toothpick into the base of each sickle.

TOOTHPICK

5) Insert the sickles into the helmet.

6) Remove the wad of newspaper and place the completed helmet on top of the basic form.

Step V: Finishing Touches

1) Use any of the etching tools to touch up and refine the completed armor.

2) Be sure all of the pieces are firmly attached, otherwise they may fall off while baking.

3) Bake in a 350° oven for 1 hour, or until hardened.

KABUTO (helmet)
and
SHŌBU (iris flower)

Instructions for making two styles of *kabuto* (helmet) and a *shōbu* (iris flower) by *origami* (paper folding) are given.

KABUTO:

The paper *kabuto* is simple to make and larger versions can be made for party hats or as part of a costume. Materials needed are:

– *Origami* paper, or any paper cut into squares (fadeless colored paper, gift wrapping paper). Avoid using thick or very thin paper because it will be difficult to make folds.

SHŌBU:

The *shōbu* is made in 3 parts: the flower, stem and leaves. Materials needed are:

– *Origami* paper in 3 sizes:

  20cm (8″) square paper for the flower

  15cm (6″) square paper for the stem

  25cm (10″) square paper for the leaves

– Scissors

– Scotch tape

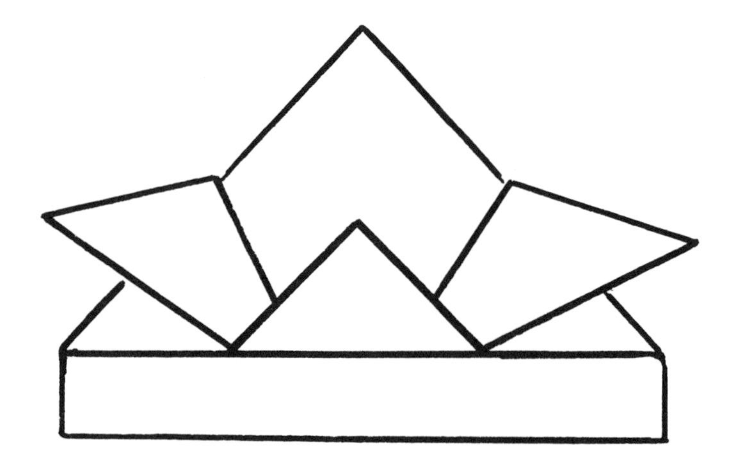

KABUTO (helmet)

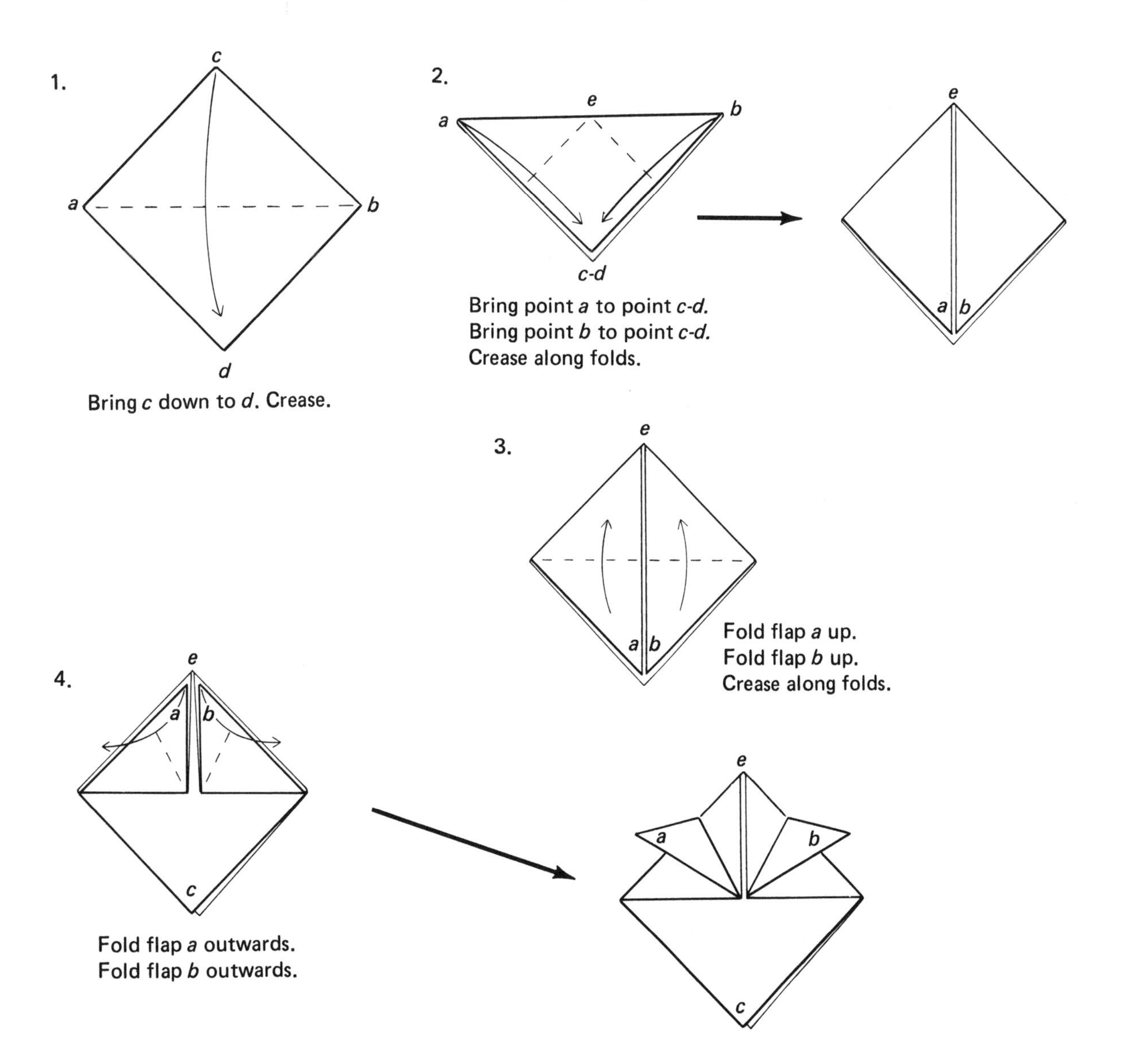

Bring *c* down to *d*. Crease.

Bring point *a* to point *c-d*.
Bring point *b* to point *c-d*.
Crease along folds.

Fold flap *a* up.
Fold flap *b* up.
Crease along folds.

Fold flap *a* outwards.
Fold flap *b* outwards.

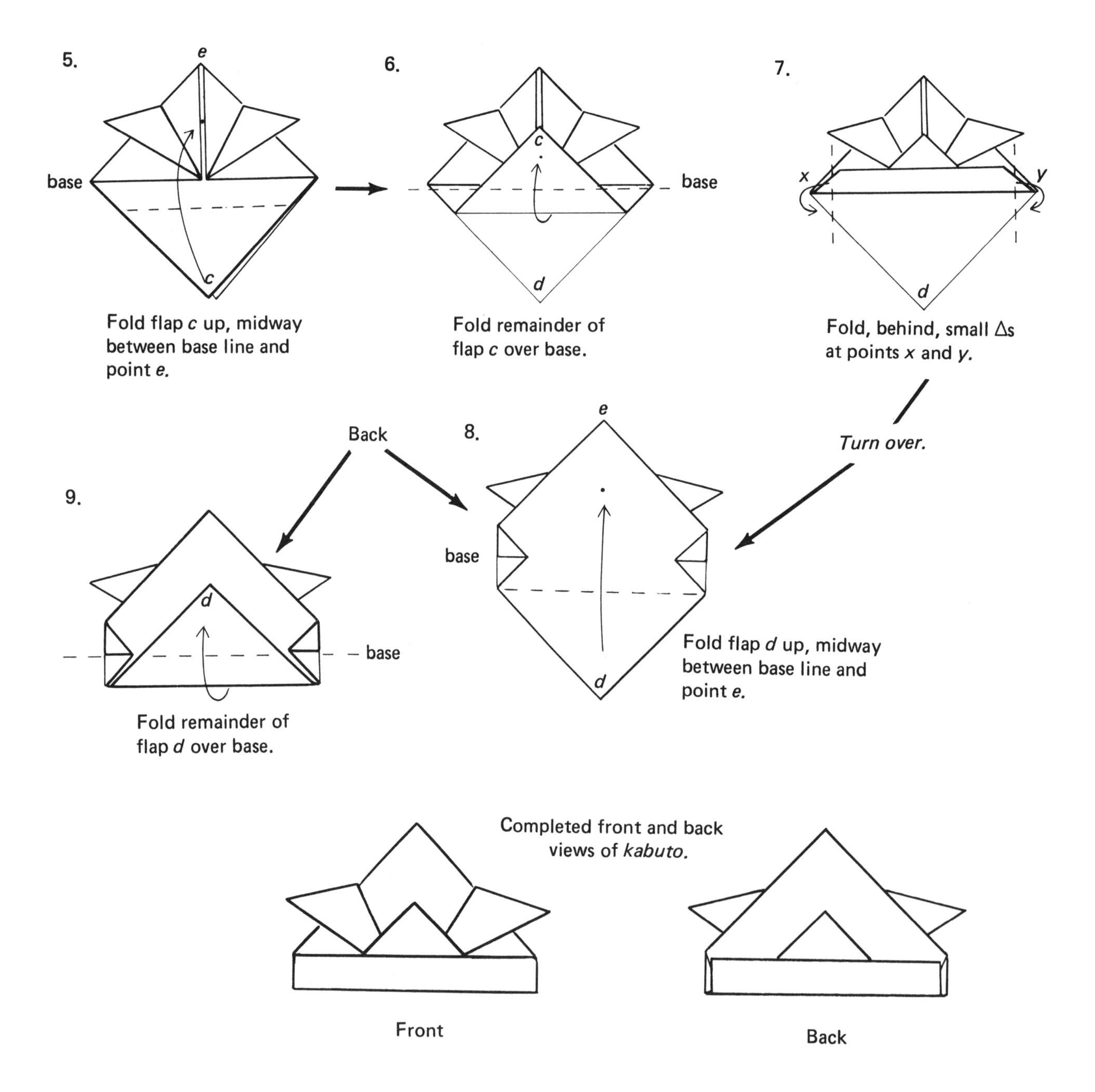
5.
e
base
c
Fold flap c up, midway between base line and point e.
6.
c
base
d
Fold remainder of flap c over base.
7.
x
y
d
Fold, behind, small Δs at points x and y.
Turn over.
Back
8.
e
base
d
Fold flap d up, midway between base line and point e.
9.
d
base
Fold remainder of flap d over base.
Completed front and back views of kabuto.
Front
Back

LONG KABUTO

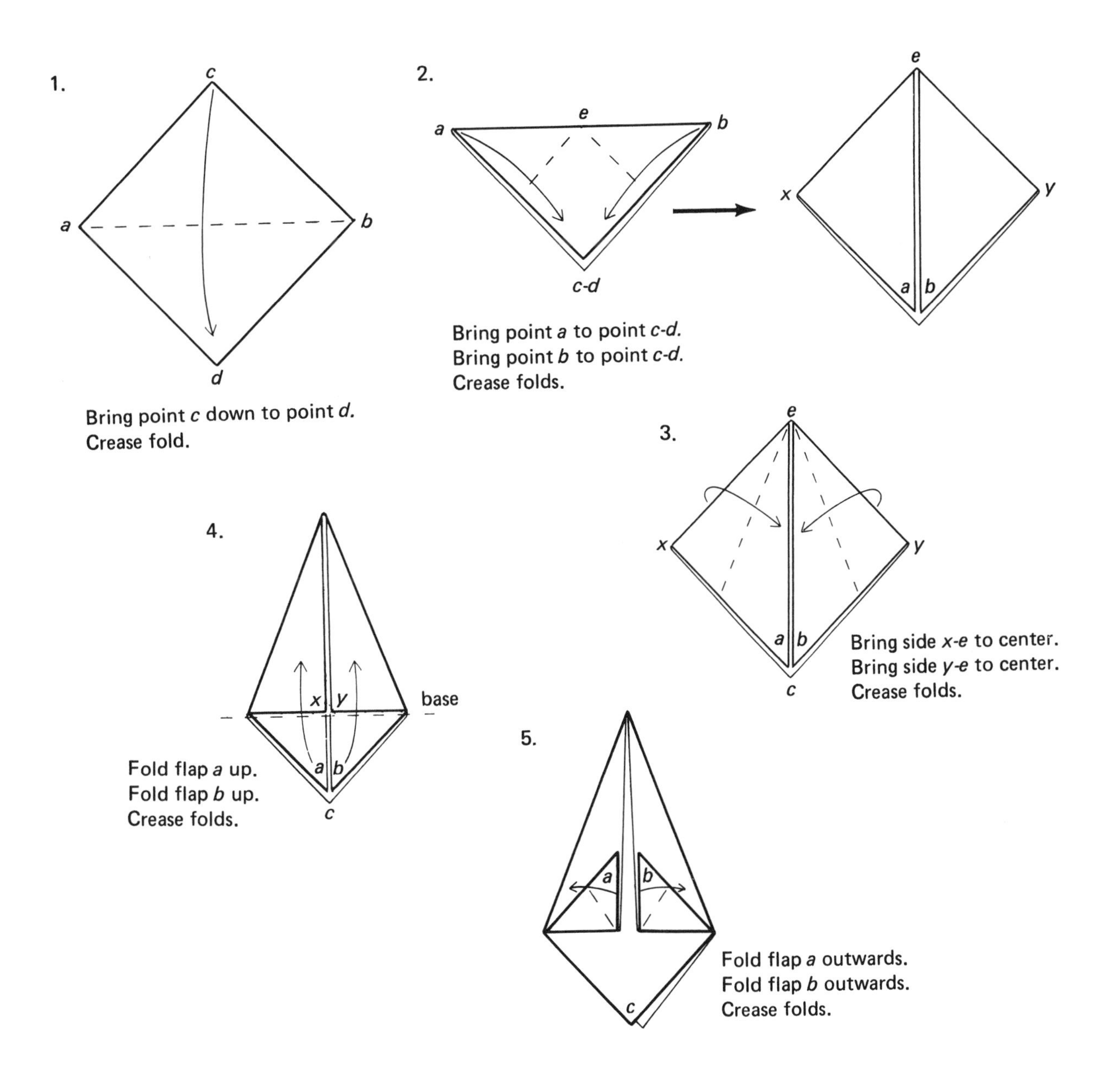
1.
c
a
b
d
Bring point *c* down to point *d*.
Crease fold.
2.
a
e
b
c-d
Bring point *a* to point *c-d*.
Bring point *b* to point *c-d*.
Crease folds.
e
x
y
a
b
3.
e
x
y
a
b
c
Bring side *x-e* to center.
Bring side *y-e* to center.
Crease folds.
4.
x
y
base
a
b
c
Fold flap *a* up.
Fold flap *b* up.
Crease folds.
5.
a
b
c
Fold flap *a* outwards.
Fold flap *b* outwards.
Crease folds.

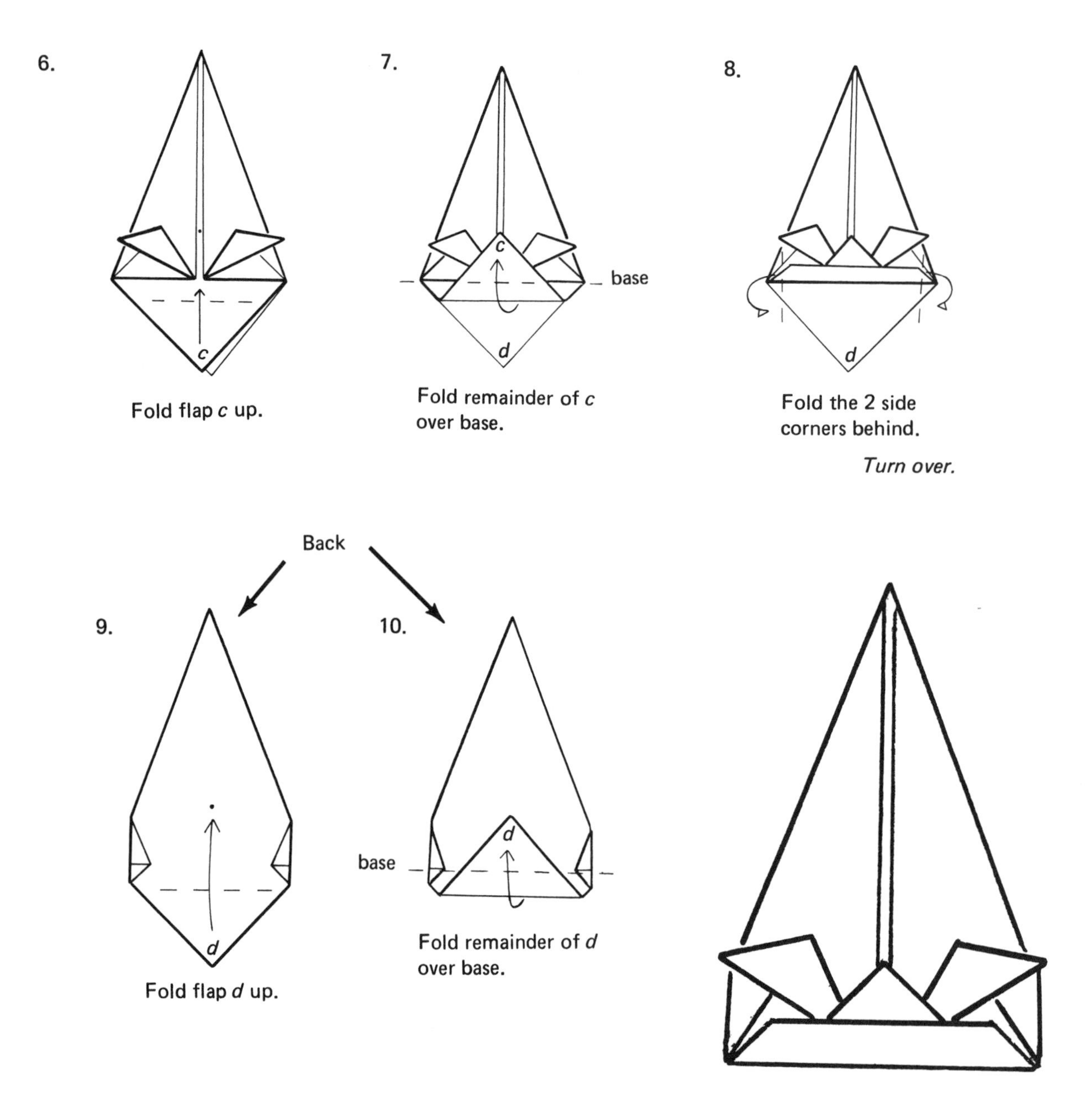
6.
c
Fold flap c up.
7.
c
base
d
Fold remainder of c
over base.
8.
d
Fold the 2 side
corners behind.
Turn over.
Back
9.
d
Fold flap d up.
10.
d
base
Fold remainder of d
over base.
Front view

SHŌBU (Iris)

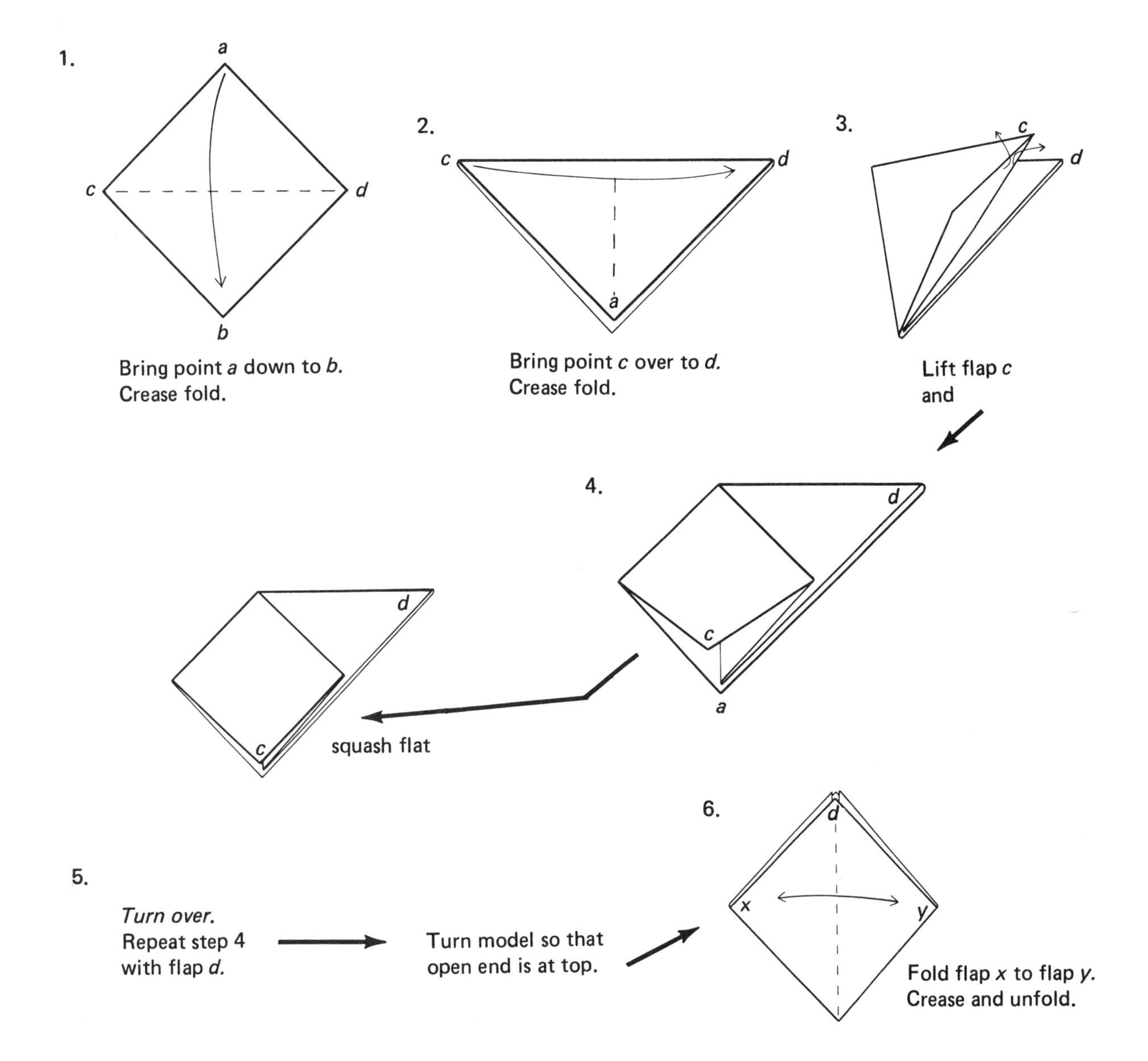

1.
a
c
d
b
Bring point *a* down to *b*.
Crease fold.
2.
c
d
a
Bring point *c* over to *d*.
Crease fold.
3.
c
d
Lift flap *c*
and
4.
d
c
a
d
c
squash flat
5.
Turn over.
Repeat step 4
with flap *d*.
Turn model so that
open end is at top.
6.
d
x
y
Fold flap *x* to flap *y*.
Crease and unfold.

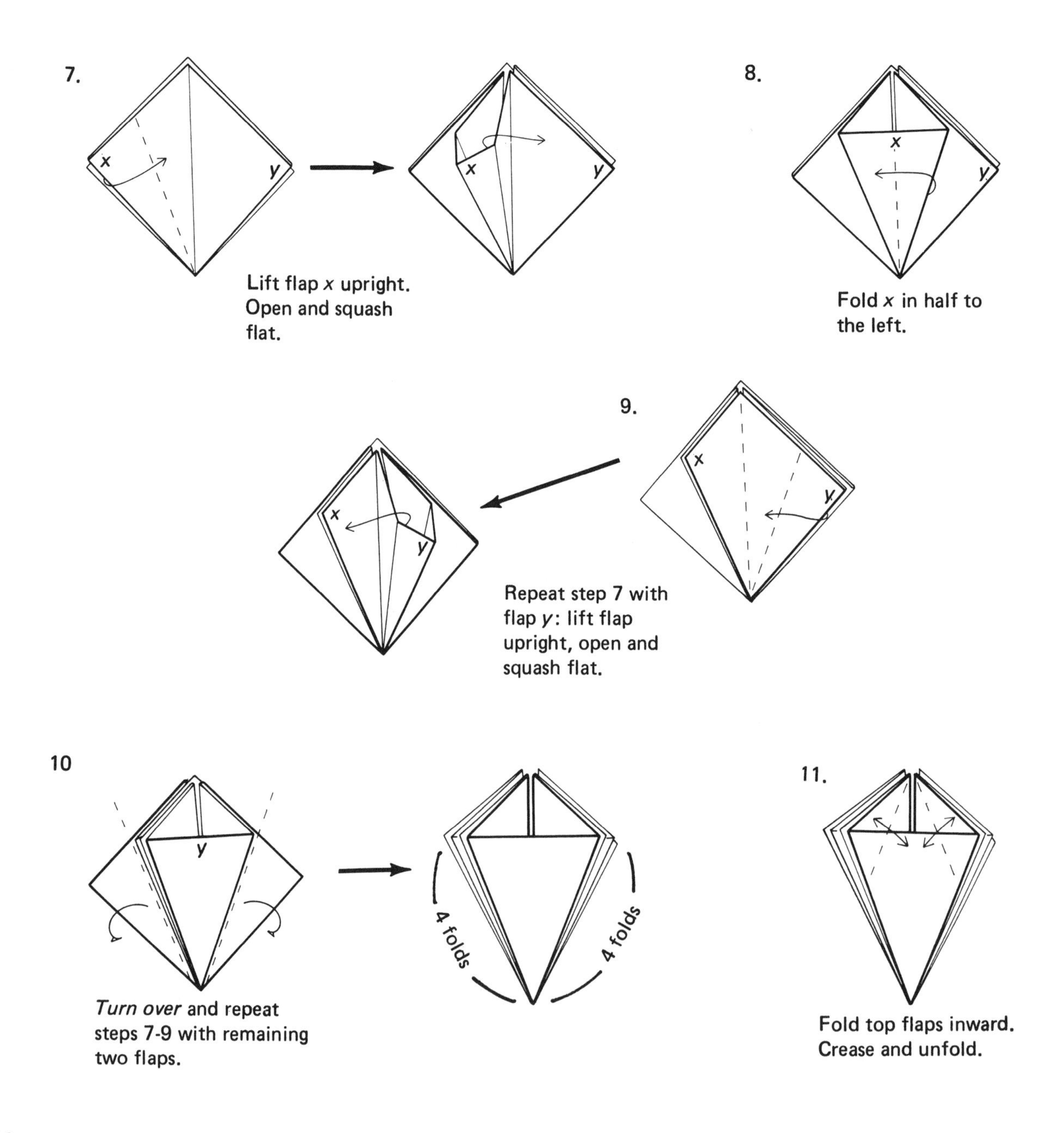

Lift flap *x* upright. Open and squash flat.

Fold *x* in half to the left.

Repeat step 7 with flap *y*: lift flap upright, open and squash flat.

Turn over and repeat steps 7-9 with remaining two flaps.

Fold top flaps inward. Crease and unfold.

12.

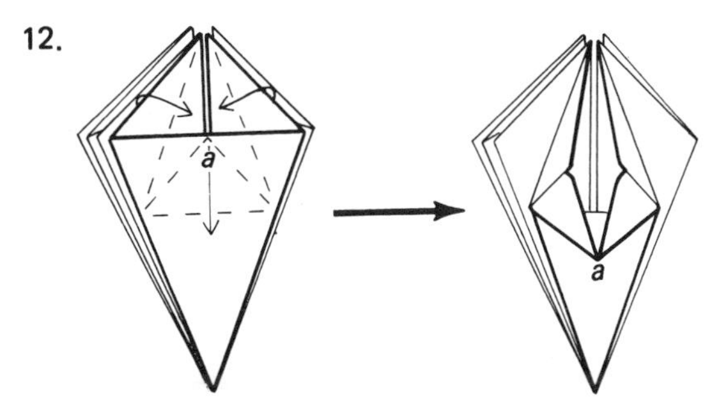

Fold 2 sides in while pulling *a* down.

13.

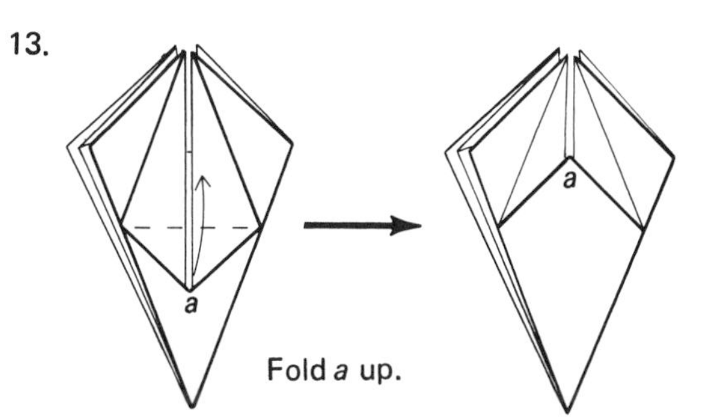

Fold *a* up.

14.

Repeat steps 11-13 on remaining 3 sides.

15.

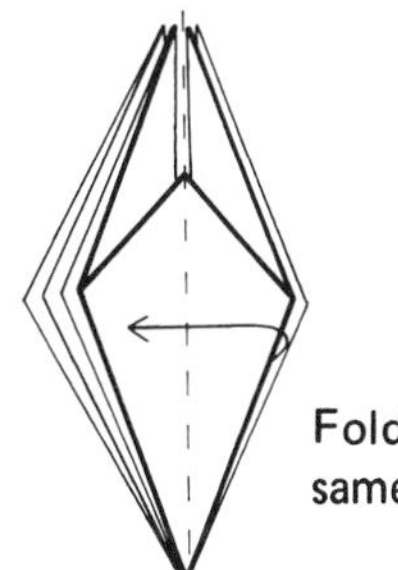

Fold in half. Do the same on other 3 sides.

16.

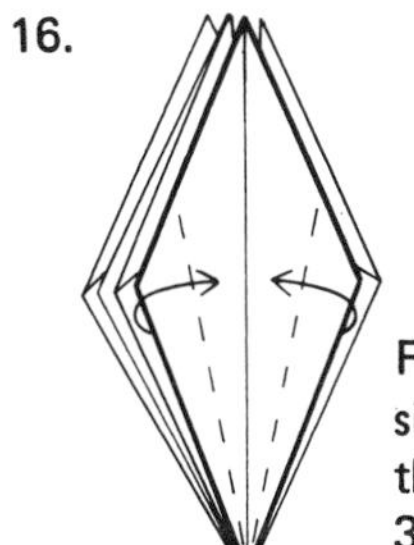

Fold along marked sides to center. Do the same with other 3 sides.

17.

Fold the 4 top flaps out to form petals.

Cut off 1/4" from tip to insert stem.

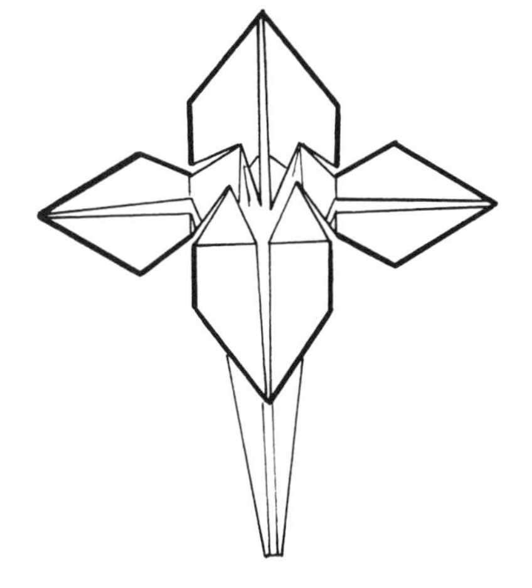

SHŌBU STEM

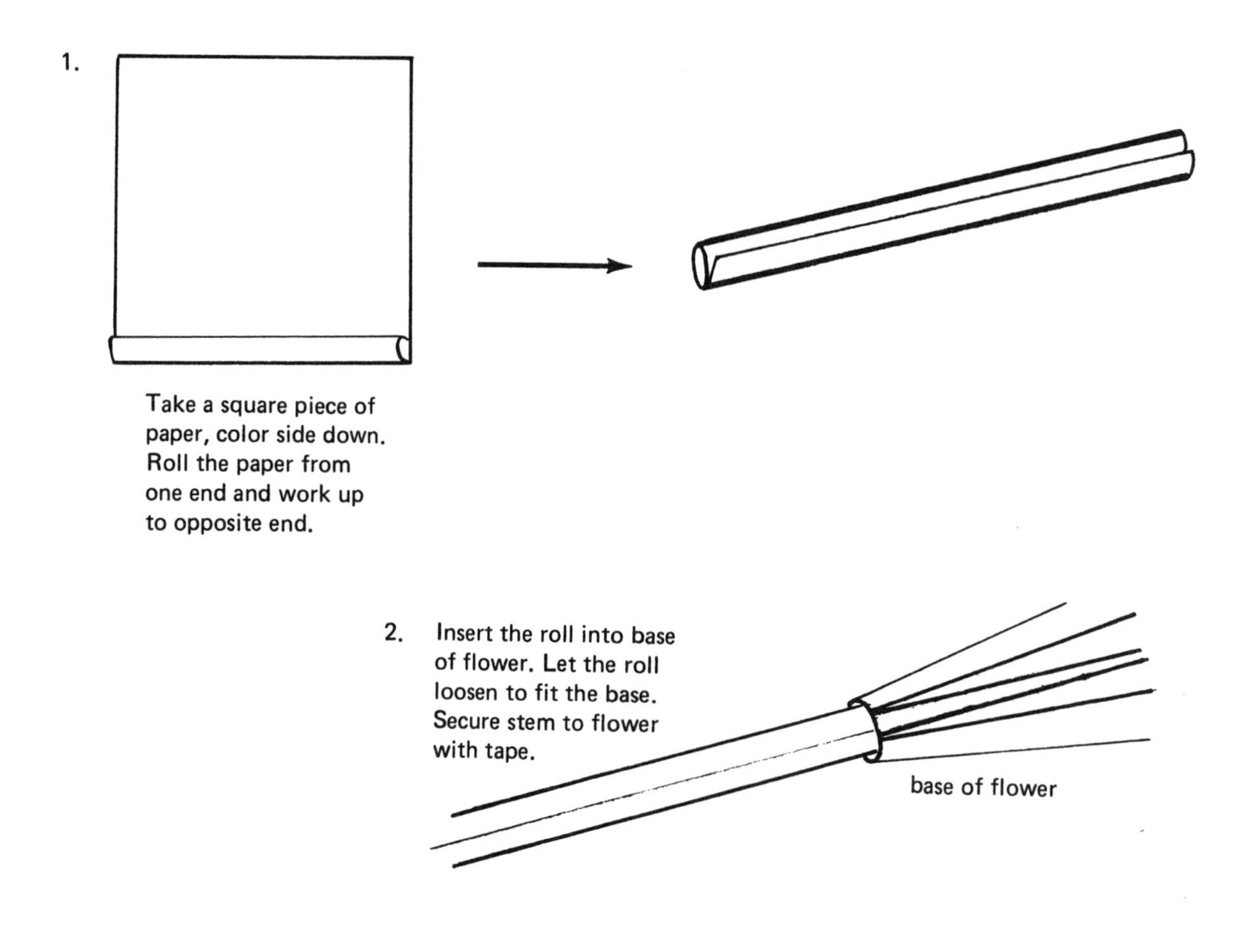

1. Take a square piece of paper, color side down. Roll the paper from one end and work up to opposite end.

2. Insert the roll into base of flower. Let the roll loosen to fit the base. Secure stem to flower with tape.

3. Tape the other end of stem and place in the center of leaves. Hold in place with tape.

SHŌBU NO HA (Iris Leaves)

1.

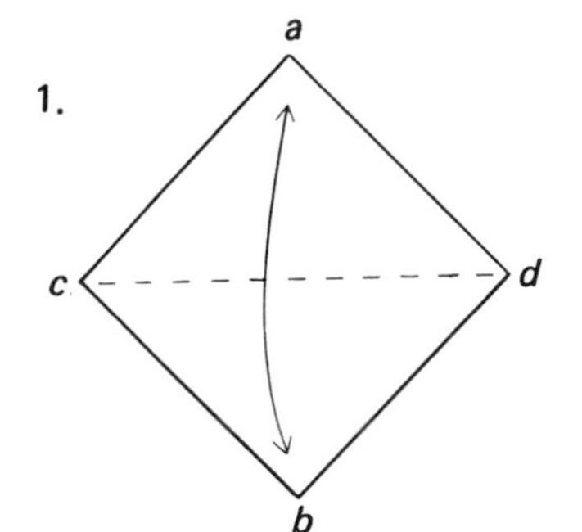

Bring *a* down to *b*.
Crease and unfold.

2.

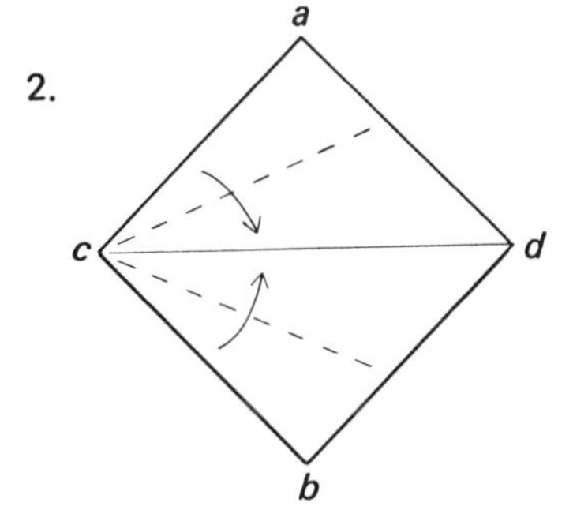

Fold side *c-a* to center.
Fold side *c-b* to center.
Crease folds.

3.

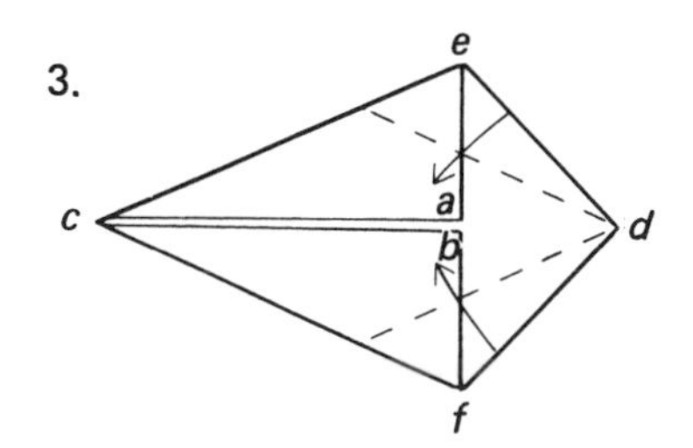

Fold side *d-e* to center.
Fold side *d-f* to center.
Crease folds.

5.

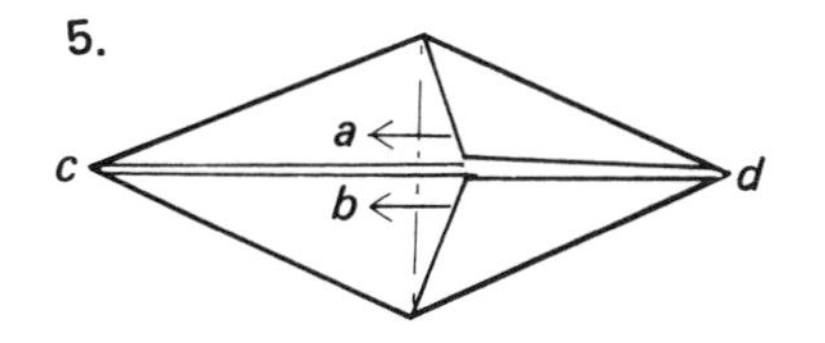

Pull *a* out and fold down.
Pull *b* out and fold down.

4.

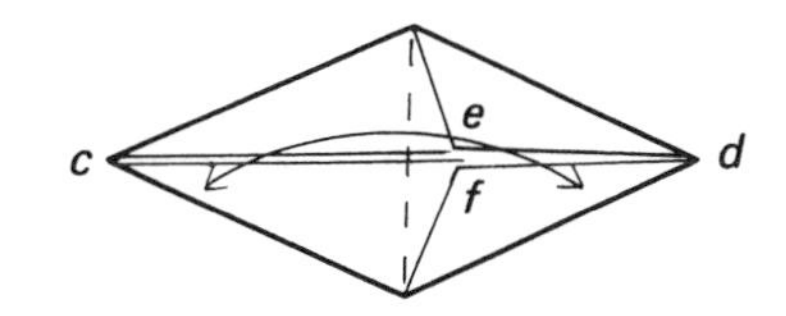

Bring *c* over to *d*.
Crease and unfold.

6.

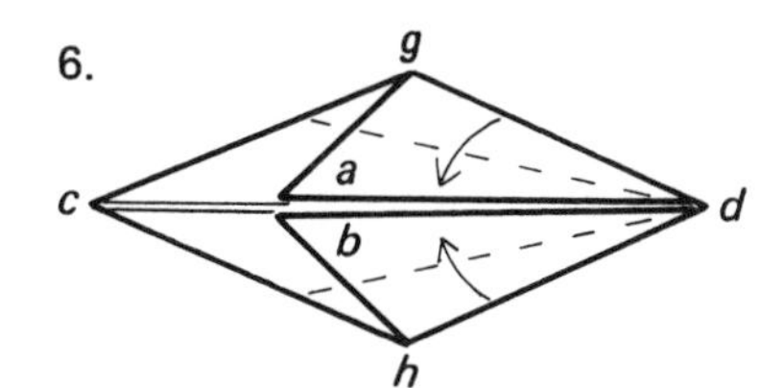

Fold side *d-g* to center.
Fold side *d-h* to center.
Crease folds.

7.

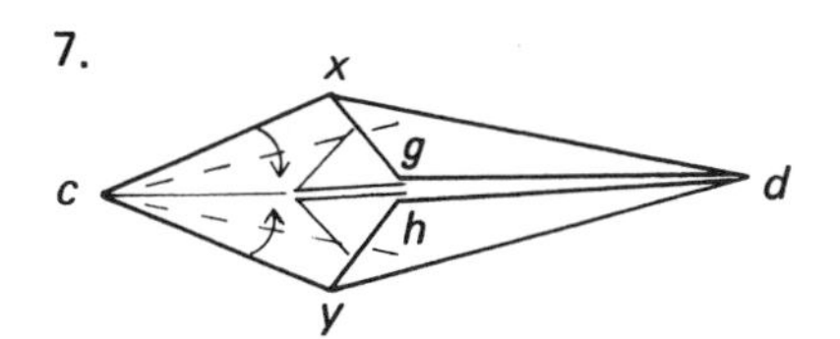

Fold side *c-x* to center.
Fold side *c-y* to center.
Crease folds.

8.

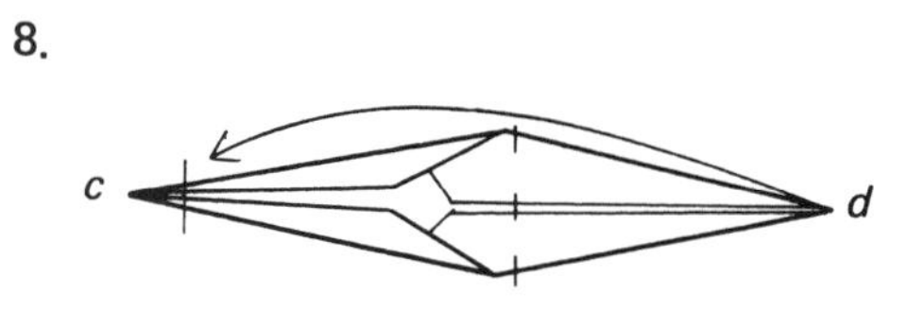

Fold *d* over, a little below *c*.

9.

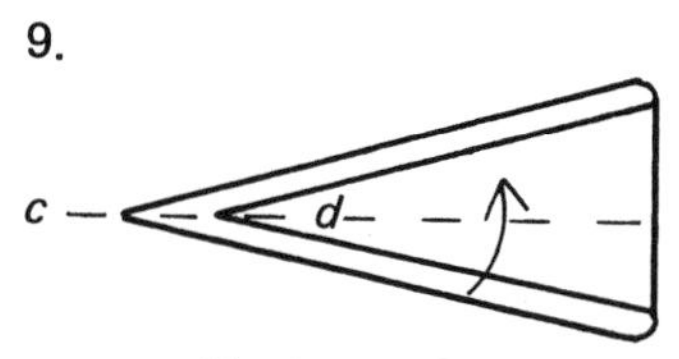

Fold in half.

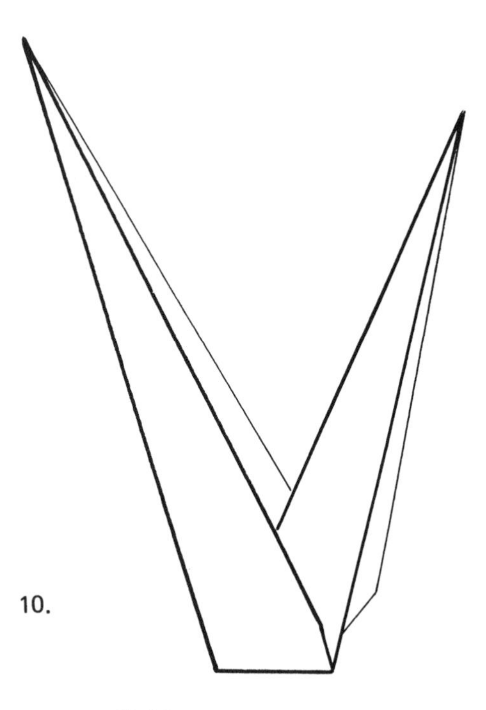

10.

Pull leaves apart.

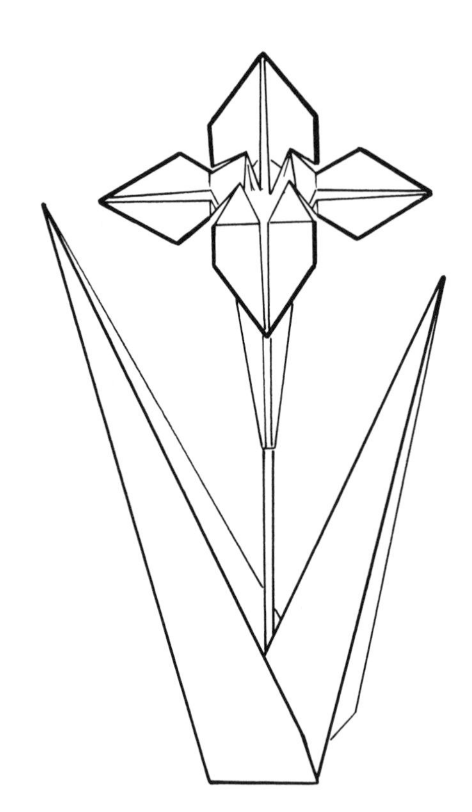

七夕

TANABATA

TANABATA

Tanabata Matsuri (Weaving Loom Festival) or, sometimes called, *Hoshi Matsuri* (Star Festival) is traditionally celebrated on the 7th day of the 7th lunar month, but is also celebrated on July 7th in some areas of Japan.

The festival was first chronicled as a national event in 755 A.D., and influenced by the writings of the poet Umeji Takehisa, it gained much popularity during the Edo Era (1603-1868).

The Festival came out of a Chinese legend about stars in the Northern Hemisphere, the Verda Star and the Altair Star, of the Lyra and Aquila constellations, approximately 15.7 light years from Earth. Shokujo (weaver - Verda Star), a daughter of a heavenly monarch, was a skillful weaver. By chance she met Kengyū (herder - Altair Star) and both fell very much in love, and wanted to marry. The king was against such a match, but after much pleading from his daughter, he finally relented. The two were so much in love and involved with each other that Shokujo began to neglect her weaving, and Kengyū, his herds. The king separated the two, placing each on opposite sides of the *Amanogawa* (Milky Way: "River of Heaven"). Shokujo pleaded with her father to allow her to meet Kengyū, which the king finally did, but they could meet only once a year, on the 7th day of the 7th lunar month.

On the first meeting day, Shokujo and Kengyū found themselves on the opposite sides of the "River of Heaven", with no bridge to unite them. The Princess wept so sadly that the crying caught the sympathy of a *kasasagi* (magpie) who with other magpies formed a bridge with their outstretched wings, enabling the couple to come together. So every year thereafter, the magpies would form the bridge. But if the night is cloudy, the legend goes, the birds will not form the bridge and the celestial lovers must wait another year before meeting.

In the United States, the celebration of *Tanabata*, held on July 7th, has been restricted to groups who gather to celebrate the meeting of the two stars with poetry writings and readings. Recently, however, organized commemoration of this festival with displays, exhibits and demonstrations has been seen in a few local Japanese American communities.

In Japan, many families celebrate the *Tanabata* festival. As is true in other festivals, symbolic decorations are used. Special bamboo trees or branches are set up in front of the house or a shrine in the garden. On the branches are hung a number of symbolic items made of paper: *tanzaku* (narrow strips of paper) on which love poems are written; *fukinagashi* (strips of different colors representing weaving); *tsuru* (crane) for long life; *fude* (brush) for improvement of calligraphy; *ami* (net) for bountiful catch in fishing or hunting and good crops; *kujikago* (lottery basket) for luck and chance; *kimono* (garment) for protection of the body; and, *kinchaku* (money pouch) for the spirit of saving. The Princess receives supplications from those who wish to improve their weaving, sewing, knowledge of music, poetry and calligraphy, all of which she is the patroness. Farmers and fishermen ask the Herder for abundance in harvest and catch.

The city of Sendai has made *Tanabata Matsuri* into a famous, elaborate celebration, held annually on August 6-8, which is in keeping with the lunar calendar. Townspeople vie with each other to decorate the main streets of the city. Residents adorn bamboo branches with strips of colored paper, streamers and other glittering material in fancy designs in front of their homes. The streamers and ribbons symbolize streaks of lightning which are common in the summer skies.

Colorful *kusudama* (balls of blossoms made from paper, cloth or celluloid with long tassels of many colors) are hung all along the streets and at the main train station. These *kusudama* mark the beginning of Sendai's *Tanabata* season.

Kusudama was originally a medicinal ball made of herbs with long threads of 5 colors attached to it. It is believed to have originated in the Heian Period (794-1192), and used to dispel evil spirits and illnesses, primarily on *Tango No Sekku*, *Hinamatsuri* and *Oshōgatsu*. Until the beginning of the 17th Century, the Emperor gave *kusudama* to invited nobility and guests in a ceremony to insure happiness and good spirits. Emperor Gomizuno-o (108th Emperor of Japan; reigned 1612-1629) discontinued this custom and, thereafter, the *kusudama* became an ornament in the households of *chōmin* (common people) and also a plaything for children.

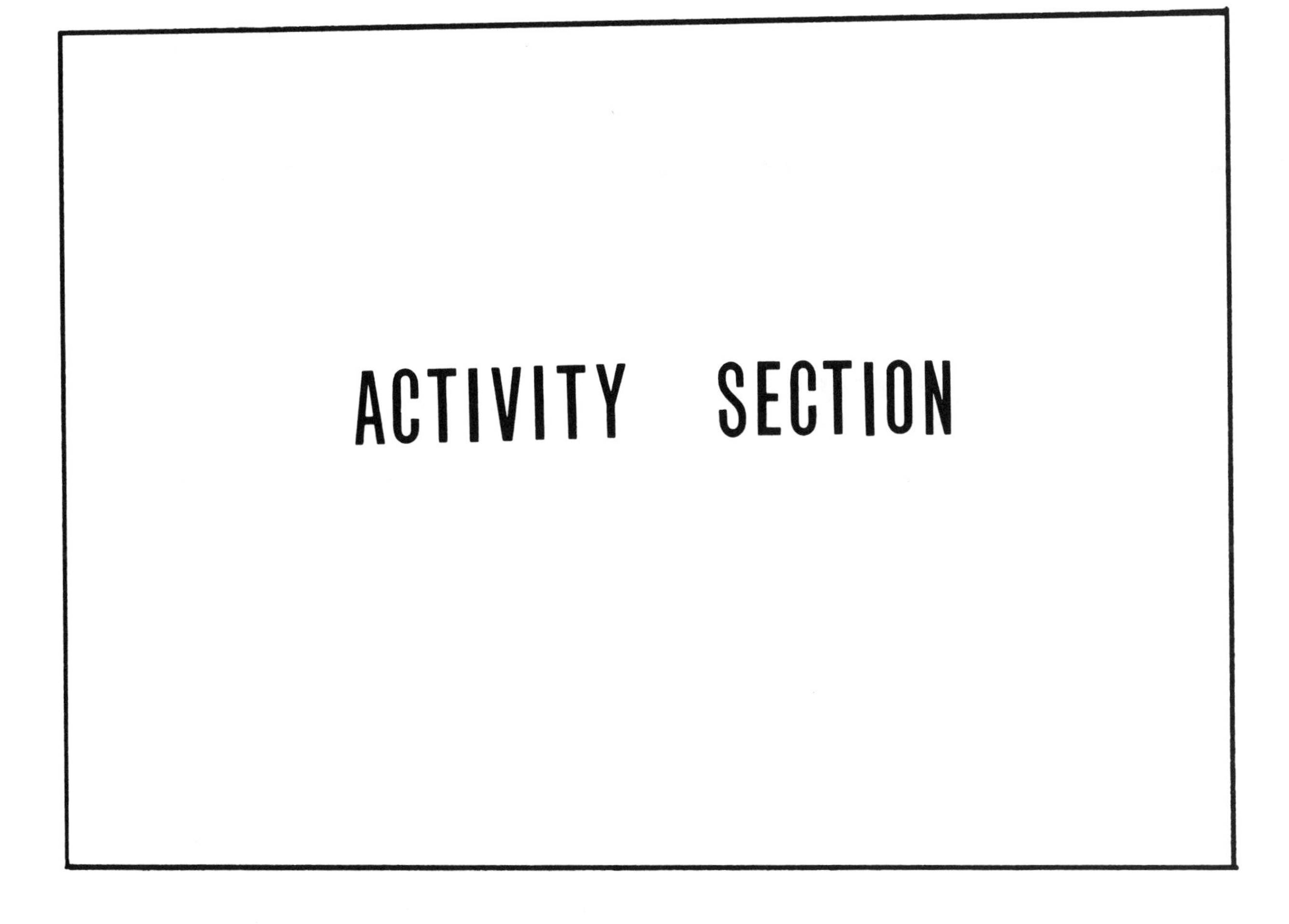

ACTIVITY SECTION

Kusudama can be hung at any festive occasion. Paper *kusudama* is easy to make using *origami* (paper folding).

MATERIALS:

- *Origami* paper, or any paper cut into squares (fadeless colored paper, gift wrapping paper). Avoid thick or very thin paper because it will be difficult to make folds.

- Scissors and small hand stapler

- 4 strands of gift wrapping ribbon, any color will do. [About 1 meter (36") per strand for an ornament the size of a grapefruit.]

- Cardboard button, 2.5cm (1") in diameter

- Heavy thread, yarn or string and needle

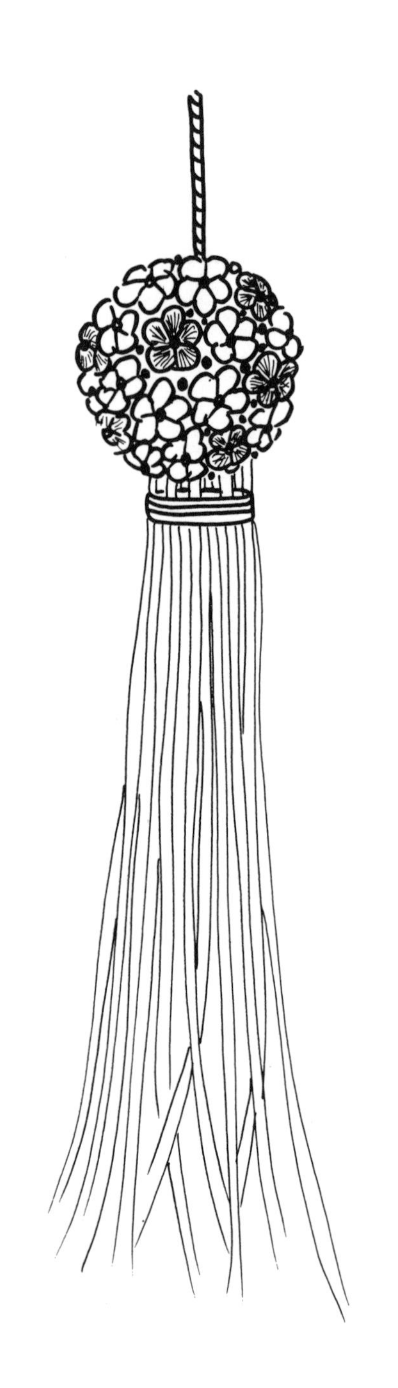

KUSUDAMA

NOTE: Use 2 pieces of paper (colored sides on outside)

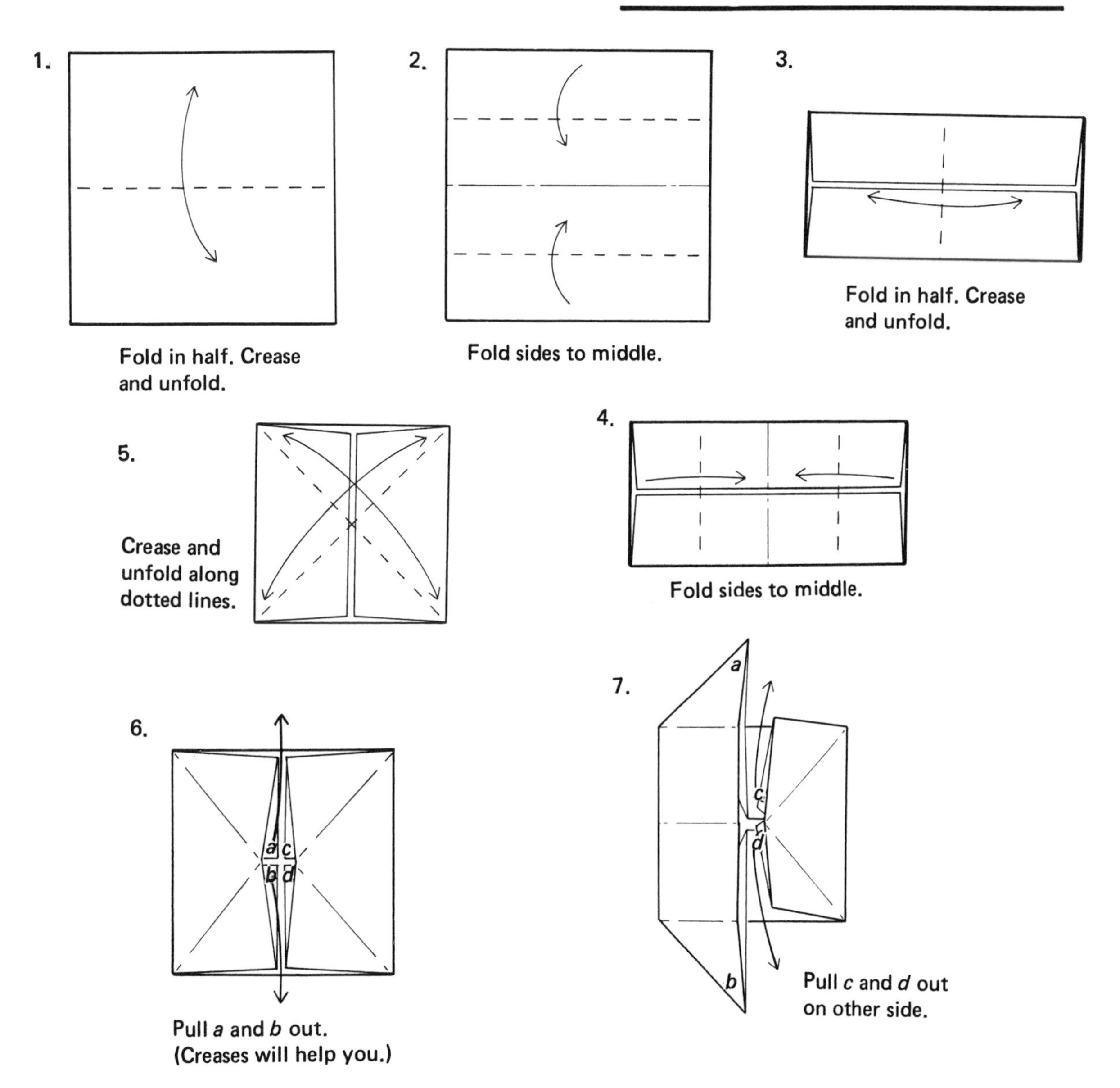

8.

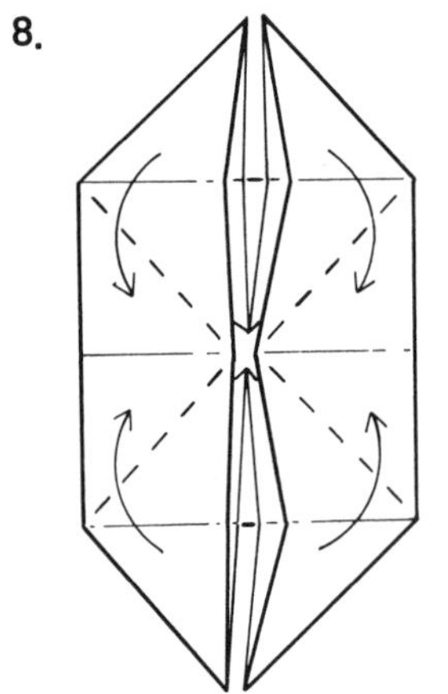

Open at *x* and squash fold each corner.

9.

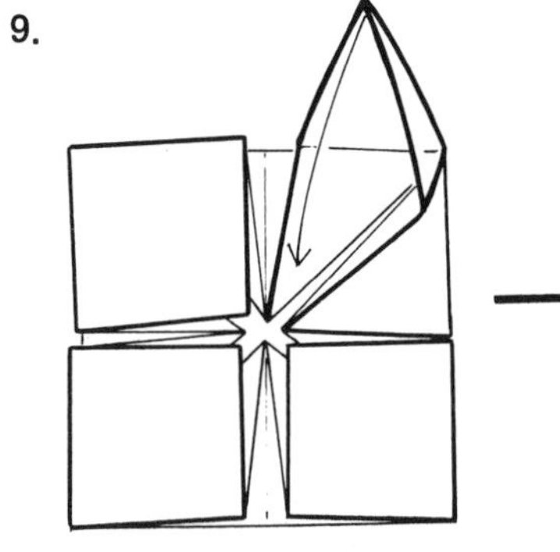

The 4 points should all meet at the center.

Fold in the 8 flaps.

10.

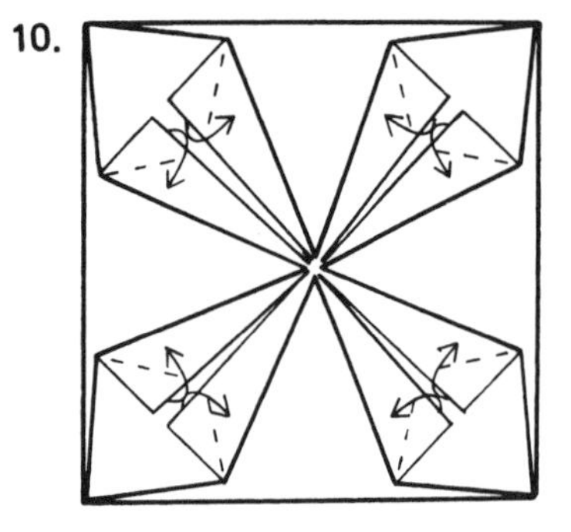

Open each of the 8 flaps at the top and squash fold to make a symmetrical triangle.

11.

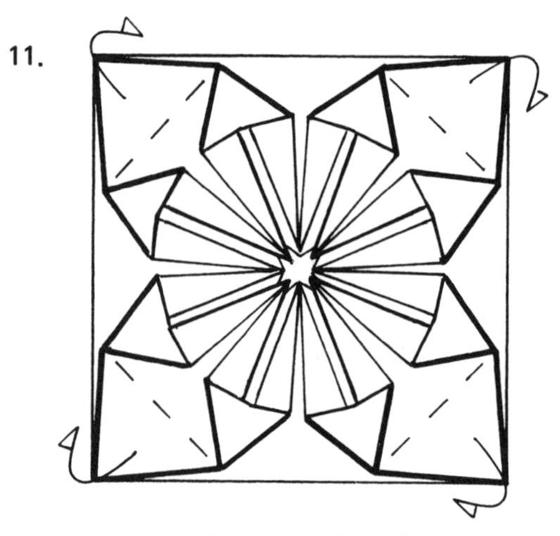

Fold each of the 4 corners back.

12.

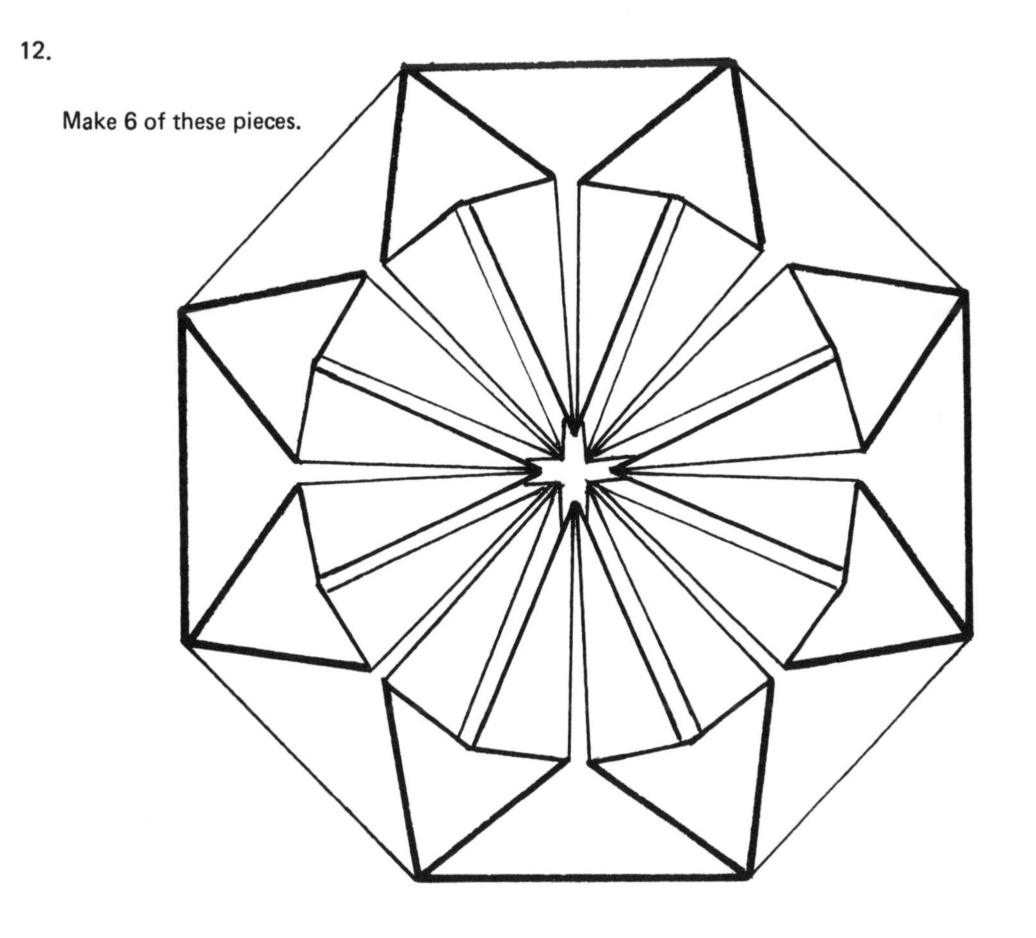

Make 6 of these pieces.

Attach the 6 pieces to each other by stapling together at each of the 4 corners (which were folded under in Figure 12) to form a "ball". *Leave one end open* through which ribbon tassel can be attached.

RIBBON TASSEL FOR KUSUDAMA

Procedure:

Step I:

Lay the ribbons flat on a table with two strands going vertically and two placed horizontally, interlaced, as illustrated below:

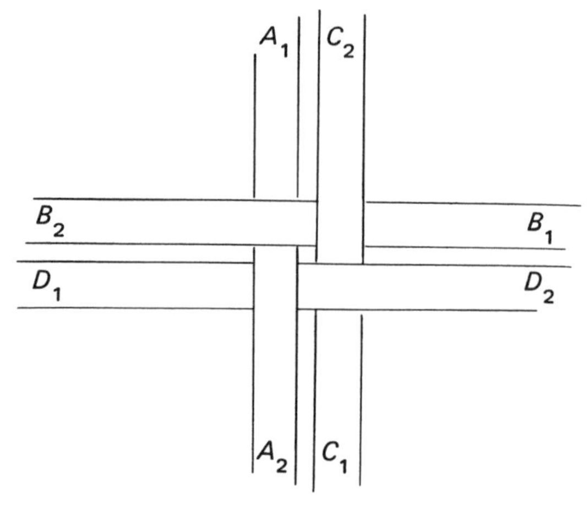

FIGURE 1

(A goes under B and then over D;

C goes over B and then under D.)

BE SURE TO ALIGN THE 4 STRANDS IN THE CENTER. Tighten all 4 strands so they touch but are not bunched up.

Step II:

Fold in this order:

1) Bring A_1 down to meet A_2.
2) B_1 crosses over to left to meet B_2.
3) C_1 goes up to meet C_2.
4) D_1 crosses over to right to meet D_2.

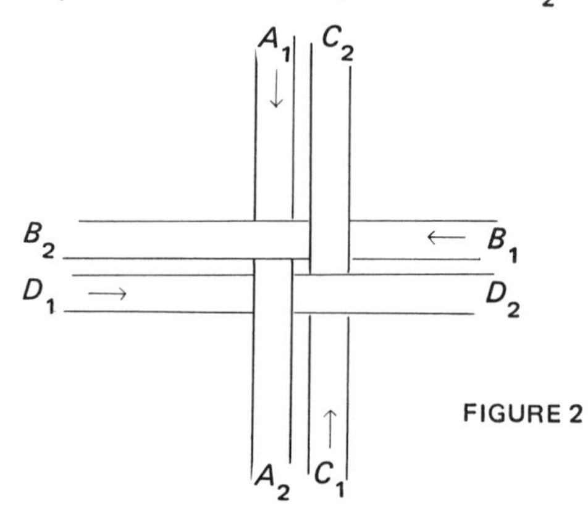

FIGURE 2

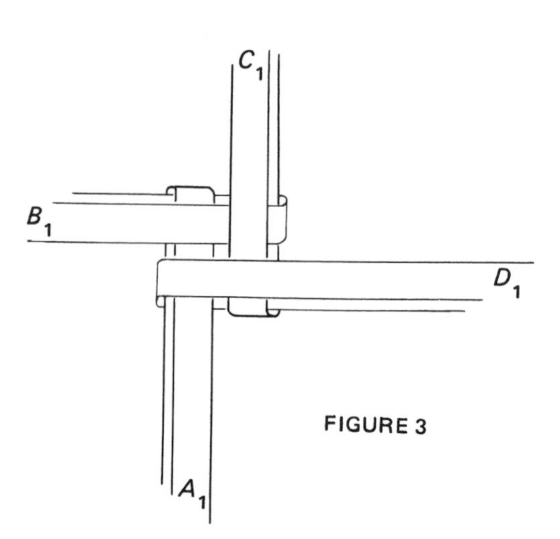

FIGURE 3

Step III:

Fold in this order:

1) Lift A_1 up, crossing over D_1 and B_1.

2) Lift B_1, crossing over C_1, to the right.

3) C_1 comes down over D_1.

4) Lift D_1 to cross over to the left; go over C_1 and weave under A_1 loop, as illustrated in Figure 5.

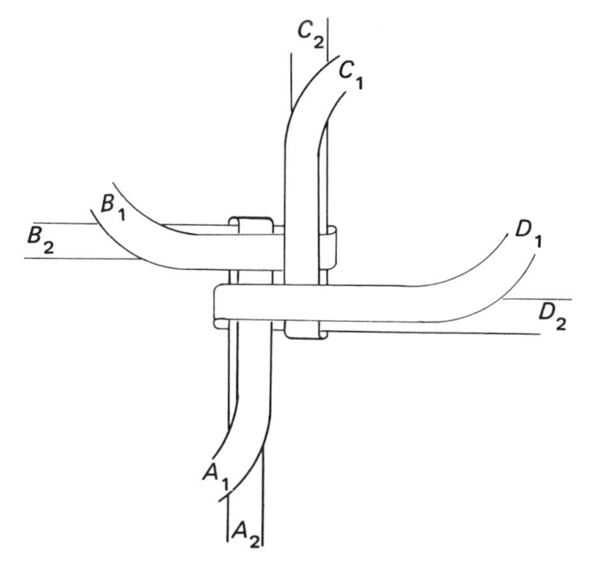

FIGURE 4

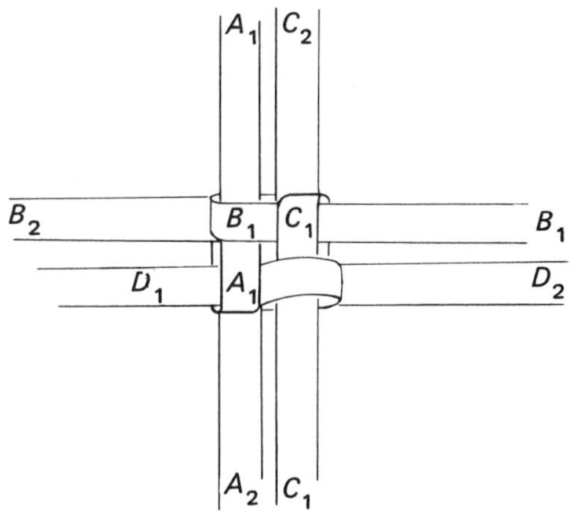

FIGURE 5

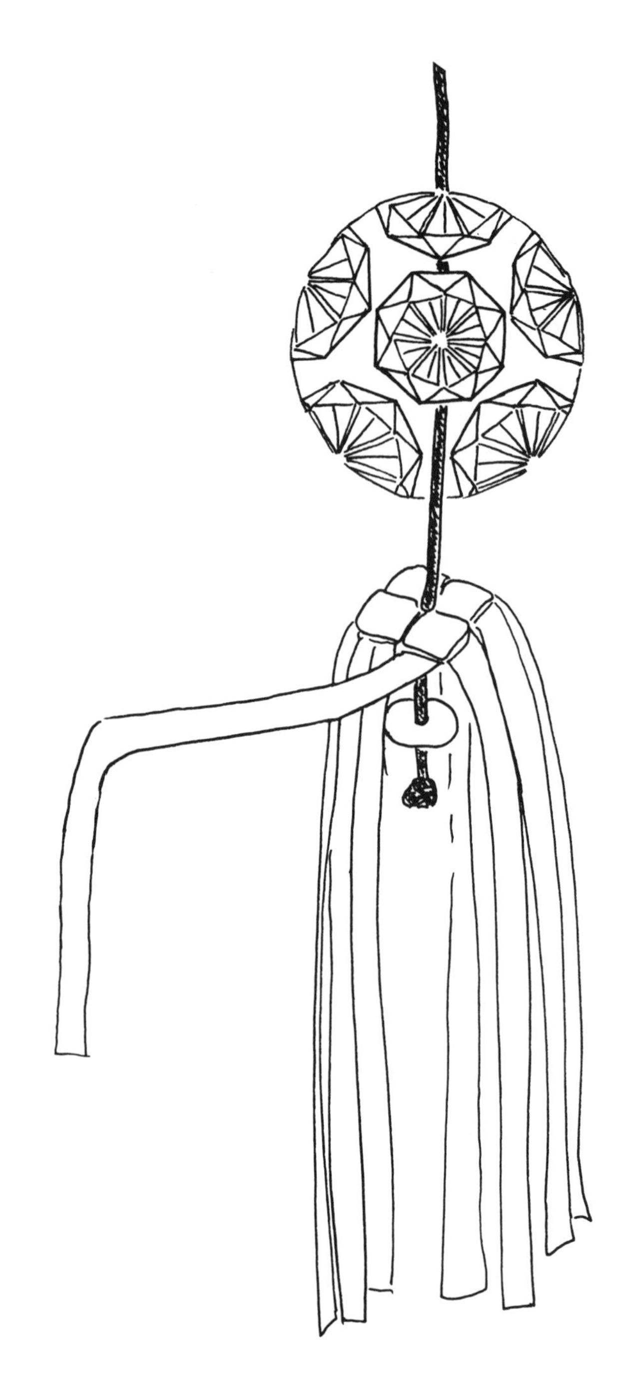

Step IV:

For reinforcement, cut out a lightweight cardboard "button". Thread through the center of "button" and woven section. Thread should be long enough to put through center of *kusudama*, with an additional 12 inches or so for suspending the *kusudama*. Yarn may be used instead of thread.

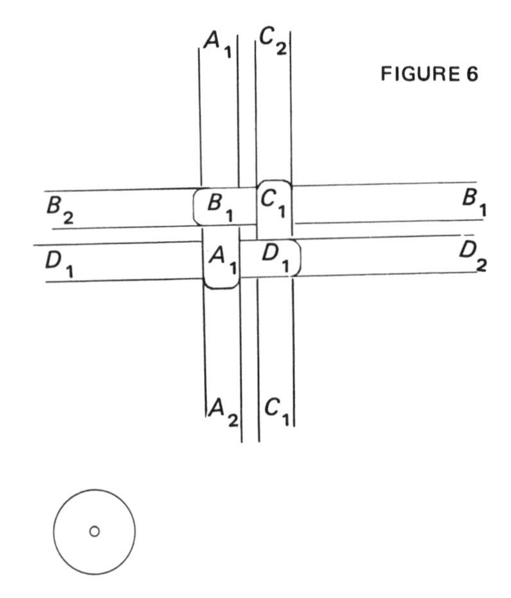

FIGURE 6

CARDBOARD "BUTTON"

BON ODORI

BON ODORI

One of the most colorful events in Japan and in the various Japanese American communities is the *Bon Odori* (*Bon* dances), a festival of community dancing, held during the summer months. *Bon* dancing might also be part of other festivals and parades.

The *Bon Odori* originated as a part of the three day Buddhist *Obon* (Festival for expression of gratitude; Feast of Lanterns), a religious celebration similar to the Christian "All Souls' Day". The early *Bon Odori* was a dance of lamentation for *Shoro-san* (spirit of the dead) where close relatives of the recently deceased would dance and sing to the beat of drums and music of the flute. From this religious beginning, the *Bon Odori* evolved to its present meaning of expressing *kimochi* (feelings), and the sharing of *kimochi* with others. *Bon Odori*, which is also referred to as *minyō* (folk singing and dancing), can be performed anytime there is a gathering. Dances reflect the unique style of music and dance of the region or village where they originated.

In the United States, various Buddhist Temples hold *Bon Odori* during July and August. A line of dancers wearing *kimono* and *yukata* (summer cotton *kimono*) dance in a circle around a huge *taiko* (drum) mounted on a platform. A variety of dances are done with the syncopated beat of the *taiko* with live or recorded music. *Uchiwa* (round, open fan), *tenugui* (hand towel), *sensu* (folding

UCHIWA

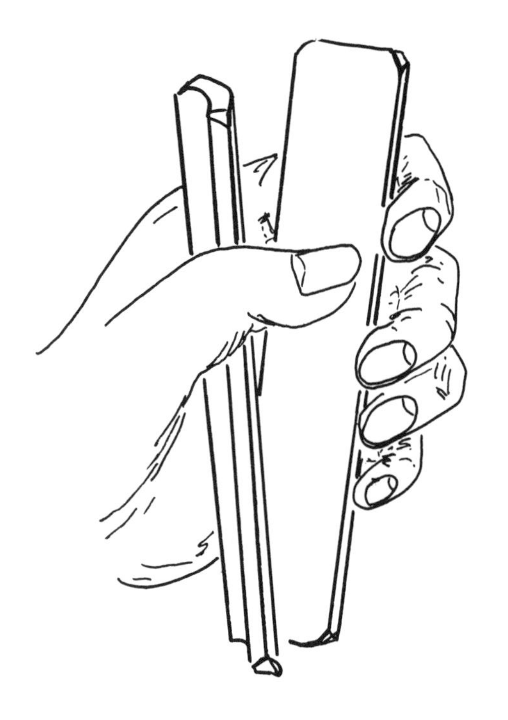

KACHI-KACHI

fan), *kachi-kachi* (hand clackers) are used in different dances.

Weeks before the *Bon Odori*, the dancers have been learning and practicing traditional dances and new *ondo* (dances to modern rhythmic melodies). Local *minyō* (folk singing/dancing) and *buyō*, (classical dance) instructors are on hand to teach. But at the actual *Bon Odori*, most anyone can join in the dancing by simply mimicking the person in front of them. These instant dancers, awkward as they sometimes are, lace the event with a community spirit of good feelings.

Bon dancing is also done in a processional style during community parades such as San Francisco's *Sakura Matsuri* and Los Angeles' *Nisei* Week.

In Japan *Obon* is celebrated during the 7th lunar month (August) from the 14th to the 16th day. For the *Bon Odori*, as well as for the dancing during the local *natsu* and *aki matsuri* (summer and autumn festivals), *yagura* (raised musicians' platforms) are built in public areas. On the night of the *Bon Odori* or the *matsuri*, beating of the drums signal the starting time. People, young and old, male and female, come together and join in the dancing and singing. Usually two or three dances are repeated throughout the evening, the rhythm and tempo getting livelier as the night goes on. Drummers take turns beating the *taiko* on the platform, each adding his or her own syncopation and style to the festivity.

Three basic types of dance/music developed in Japan: *kagura, dengaku* and *furyū*. Although it is from *furyū* that *Bon* dancing seems to have derived, it is of interest to see the nature of all three types.

KAGURA

The original *kagura* (sacred *Shinto* music and dance) is believed to be the dance and song performed by the goddess, Ame-no-uzume-no-mikoto, when she was able to entice the sun-goddess, Amaterasu-ōmikami out of the cave of Ama-no-Iwato. This performance is considered the prototype of the many kinds of *kagura* performed at *Shinto* shrines by *miko* (shrine maidens) as offerings of prayer for harvest and blessings. These dances are slow and majestic in style, with emphasis on the reverence of nature.

Kagura has also been an important feature of the Japanese Court. By the Heian Era (794-1192), the introduction of Chinese musical instruments influenced *kagura* and it became known as *gagaku* (Court music), which to this day is performed by the Imperial Household Agency in exactly the same form as centuries before. Instrumental performance of the *gagaku* is called *kangen*, and when performed with dance drama, it is called *bugaku*.

DENGAKU

Dengaku, translated as rice-paddy music, occur in three forms. The earliest form, *sangaku*, is not indigenous to Japan, but was brought over by wandering minstrels or performing troops from Central Asia traveling province to province in Japan, performing pantomines, acrobatics, comic mimicry, juggling and puppetry. They were accompanied by music created on the *binzasara* and *surizara*, wooden percussion type instruments.

The other two forms of *dengaku* derived from the earlier *sangaku. Sarugaku* developed as a blend of *sangaku* and *bugaku* (dance drama). *Ta-asobi* developed as a simpler form of *sangaku* as local amateurs imitated the traveling minstrels. Regional and local legends and stories were infused into *ta-asobi*, and local dialects were preserved through the narration and chants that accompanied the performance.

These three forms of *dengaku* are considered the forerunners of the Japanese dance drama, *noh*, which developed under the patronage of the Shōgun Ashikaga Yoshimitsu (1367-1395).

FURYŪ

Furyū means to drift and float about. One early example of this type of dance/music was the Buddhist gatherings, after religious services, during which people and priests would dance for enjoyment, accompanied at times by *kane* (gong). Another expression was the *odori-nembutsu*, which originated in the Heian Period (794-1192) and was encouraged by Kuya (Kōya) Shonin (903-972). These types of ritual dance, free movements (dancing) to the recitation of sutras accompanied by the *fue* (flute), *taiko* (drum) and *kane* (gong), were performed as an expression of gratitude. They are believed to be the forerunner of the religious *Bon Odori*, which is also classified as a form of *furyū*.

The early form of *Bon Odori* (dance of lamentation) was later influenced by simple folk dancing which had already developed as expressions of joy, sorrow, hopes and desires in life. Folk dancing was performed during regional festivals, many of which coincided with the religious *Obon*. Over the years, fusion of festivals took place and in this manner, *Bon Odori*, which began as a religious mass for the spirits of the dead, evolved into a gala festival of dancing with good spirit and fun.

Villages and regions developed their own dance and music styles (collectively called *Matsuri Bayashi*. Two other music/dance styles are the well-known *Gion Bayashi*, an elegant and stately form accompanied by an orchestra, which developed in Kyoto and *Kanda Bayashi*, characterized by its gay and free form, which originated in Edo (Tokyo).

The development and performance of *Bon Odori* was encouraged and fostered by the *tono-sama* (feudal lords) during the Tokugawa Era (1603-1868). Two of the more famous *Bon Odori* gatherings, renown for the numbers of participants, are the *Awa Odori* of Tokushima City and the *Gujo Odori* of Gifu Prefecture. The *Awa Odori* is a processional style of dance, going through the streets of the city. It originated as a welcome to the Lord of Tokushima. The *Gujo Odori* is danced in a large circle. This *Bon Odori* was sponsored and financially supported by the ruling Aoyama clan of Gifu Prefecture, who originated this gathering as a way to promote goodwill among the farming and merchant classes.

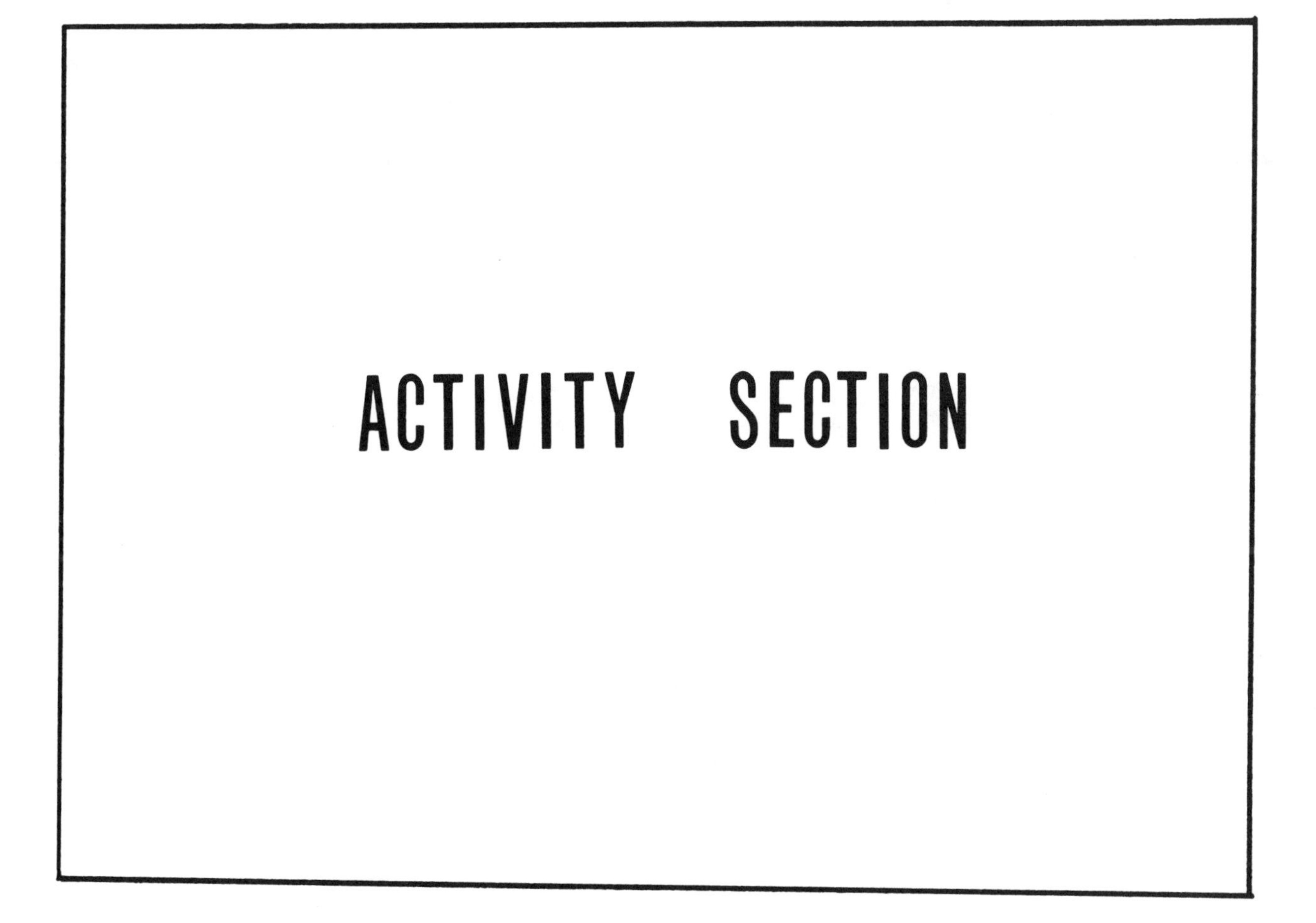

ACTIVITY SECTION

BON ODORI

There are many varieties of *Bon Odori*, some becoming famous and popular and spreading throughout Japan. One of the most famous dances is *Tankō Bushi*, Coal Miner's Song of Kyūshū. The music and dance steps are both given. The rhythmic beat and steps make it relatively easy to learn. A recording of the music can be purchased at a Japanese music or bookstore in various communities. Be sure to ask specifically for *Kyūshū Tankō Bushi*, as there are several coal miner's songs.

YAGURA

TANKŌ BUSHI

Tankō Bushi, Coal Miner's Song of Kyūshū: This dance is done in a circle, with the participants moving counterclockwise. The sequence of steps are done repeatedly following the rhythm of the song.

No. of Beats	Hand and Body Movements	Feet Positions
(per action)	Clap hands to tempo of music until lyrics begin.	Both feet together. 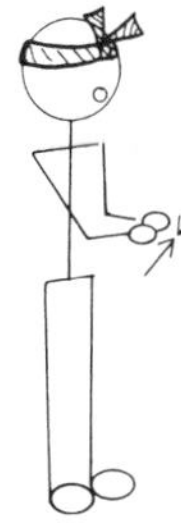
Begin dancing with lyrics 4 Beats	1) Both arms and hands to right side of body as if holding a shovel. Make 2 up and down digging motions, coordinating hands and feet movement. 	1) Right foot forward, taps twice to rhythm.
4 Beats	2) Repeat above motions (No. 1) to the left side. 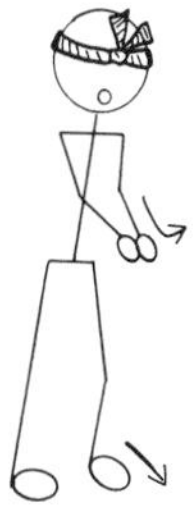	2) Left foot forward, taps twice to rhythm.

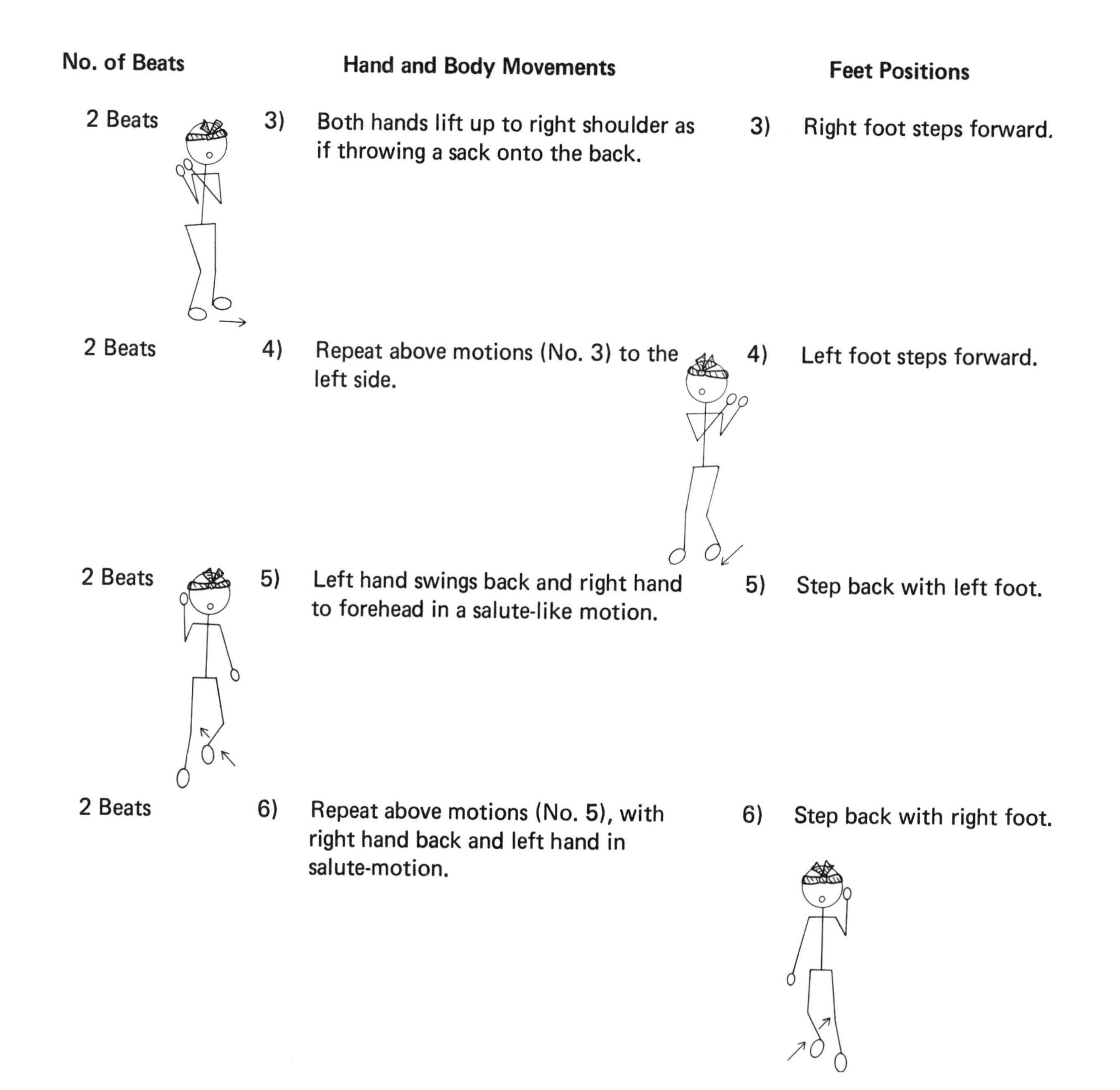

No. of Beats	Hand and Body Movements	Feet Positions
2 Beats	3) Both hands lift up to right shoulder as if throwing a sack onto the back.	3) Right foot steps forward.
2 Beats	4) Repeat above motions (No. 3) to the left side.	4) Left foot steps forward.
2 Beats	5) Left hand swings back and right hand to forehead in a salute-like motion.	5) Step back with left foot.
2 Beats	6) Repeat above motions (No. 5), with right hand back and left hand in salute-motion.	6) Step back with right foot.

No. of Beats	Hand and Body Movements	Feet Positions
4 Beats 	7) Both hands push forward from chest level and pulls back, and pushes forward again.	7) Starting with right foot, step forward with each arm "push".
2 Beats 	8) Body leans forward slightly as hands cross in front (a) and uncrossing to the sides as if clearing away bushes (b). The body motion swings forward and back with the crossing and uncross-ing of the hand/arm movement.	8) Right foot forward, with the weight of the body going forward and then back onto the left foot, co-ordinating it with the crossing of the arms.
4 Beats	9) Clap hands 2 times, 1 clap to 2 beats.	9) Both feet together 

Start sequence from No. 1 through No. 9, following the tempo of the music and continue to repeat until the end of song.

Kyūshū TANKŌ BUSHI
G C
TSU-U KI GA DE- TA DE - TA TSU-KI GA DE- TA
Em G
--- A YOI - YOI MI - I - KE - TA - AN - KO NO ---
D G
--- U - E NI --- DE - TA A - AN MA - RI --- EN-TO-
C D G
TSU GA --- TA - KA - I --- NO DE SA --- ZO-YA-
D C G C D
- OTSU-KI SA - AN KE - MU - TA --- KA RO SA-NO YOI-YOI.

INDEX

JANE M. HORII – is involved in primary education (has taught in Japan, Bermuda and San Francisco) and presently at the Nueva Day School and Learning Center, Hillsborough, California. Her studies and travels have taken her to England, Mexico, Hong Kong, Bangkok, Singapore, Taiwan and various States. Her next adventure is Peru.

NANCY K. (MORIGUCHI) ARAKI – has been involved in the area of human relations/multi-cultural education in the San Mateo City and San Francisco School Districts. Presently she is writing curriculum and works as a consultant in multi-cultural education. Her other interests are acting, Gagaku, and multi-media productions.

This book is not the first joint venture for these two. Usually Jane and Nancy have paired as an almost unbeatable doubles team in ping pong.